More About This

More About This...

Metaphysical Thoughts and Questions of the Heart

Essays

Victoria Chames

Other books by this author
Inchworms: Poems, Sketches, and Stories
A Space Between Rains: Love Poems About Endings and Beginnings
Victory Is My Name, A Memoir, Book One: The Burning-Barrel

©2019 by Victoria Chames. All rights reserved.
No part of this book may be reproduced in any
form without written consent except for quotations
of brief passages used in articles, critiques, or
reviews.
978-1-7359781-0-9
MAT-081825cx2+

Published in the United States
Darkhorse Press U.S.
Oakland, California

Zen... does not confuse spirituality with thinking about God while one is peeling potatoes. Zen spirituality is just to peel the potatoes.

- Alan Watts

Table of Contents

Unlearning	1
The Truth	4
Looking For Grace	6
No Mistakes	10
How You See It	13
Courage and Faith	15
Writing From Within	16
Snapshot	17
We Are Revealed	18
FYI, I love You	19
The Darkness / Let It Be	20
Mothers	23
How To Write The Hard Stuff	28
Into The Light	30
The Edge Of Reality	31
Rain Thoughts	34
Query Letters and Cowboy Boots	38
I Don't Know A Thing About Love	42
Who We Are	44
Writing Green	48
How To Retire	50
Writing Your Memoir	53
The Writer's Calling	56

The Path/ Life After Life 58

Carousel and Candle 60

Telling The Truth 61

The Way 62

All I Truly Am 63

Bridges/ Changes 65

Grace, The Gift Unasked For 67

Remembering The Winters 68

Roberto 69

Saying Yes To Your Calling 71

TheNorth Shore 72

Believe Anyway 74

Macho/ Macha 77

Forgiving... 79

The Little Gifts 82

The Leap 84

Compass Points.. 87

We Who Have Come Here 89

Little Bird In The Backyard This Morning

Introduction

In her book, The Right To Write, author Julia Cameron says, "We should write because we are writers, whether we call ourselves that or not." She says this about everyone, and "It is "our natural birthright, a spiritual inheritance." And she declares for those of us who still doubt, "Higher forces speak to us through writing."

Written words are more powerful than the spoken kind. They don't just hang suspended in the air for a moment and then disappear, they stay. A book, a letter, a sketch on a scrap of paper, these are tangible things. They exist in physical form that can travel, and the truths they hold can be shared in many places by many minds for centuries, even millennia. Words are undeniably powerful. The best and the worst of human beings, gentle saints and brutal dictators, have used words to influence the parts of humanity that their ideas resonated with.

Words that are true can help and heal wounds that we may share with many others unknowingly, and knowing comforts us with the reassurance that we are not alone.

It is said, "Actions speak louder than words," and this is true, up to a point. They are louder, but not better. Violence seems more powerful than words, and actions appear more forcefully effective, but only for a flash in time. Words are a more lasting medium to express things like truth, courage, compassion, and a simpler kind of love for ourselves and our species. They show us what these things look like, and once we see, we are better able to choose what we want to be in this life.

Words written down reach farther into the world, and hold their meaning through changes. What is true, once told, can never be undone. What is true is eternal, and once told, it is no longer a secret. Whatever the circumstances, whoever finds the truth and knows it, is already free.

1. Unlearning

It was the summer I was ten years old and the warm lazy days flowed along so easy and carried me with them and there was plenty of time. That was when I first started to look at the world around me and to notice things beyond the end of my own nose. Sometimes when I was by myself I climbed up into the little pear tree and sat in the branches and wondered about things like life and God.

I'd be wondering about what God was, but then I'd notice a perfect green pear I could pick, so I did. And I ate the pear and it was warm from the sun, and crunchy and sour and sweet at the same time, and the juice ran down my chin and I forgot all about God. Everything was good, and God was taking care of it, and that was enough for me.

I knew that God was around, watching out for me, just like Granny said, keeping me safe. Summer evenings when I went to bed and it wasn't even dark yet, I looked out my window at the lavender-colored sky above the roofs, and I understood that God was a something that filled the whole twilight sky, that kept the whole world in order, and still had time to notice me falling asleep. God was like the sky except bigger, and He was also a someone, that saw me and knew me and loved me and He thought I was okay, even if somebody else said I wasn't.

I came to wish with all my young heart that I could be the same person on the outside as I was on the inside, just be me, and that would be okay with everybody else. But I didn't dare.

Then I grew up and followed the rules even though it was hard, because they mostly didn't seem very fair. The simple truth is, at the bottom of all truths, most of us just want to be who we really are, but it's hard to know what that is, because most of the people in our world want us to be everything else but that.

When we were first learning what life was like and what we were supposed to be, we each got taught a system of well-meaning lies, like: "You're not as smart... You're not as pretty... You're not good enough unless..." And worst of all, "You can't do that, you can't be that, and you shouldn't even want that, because... (fill in the blank.) For me, the worst untruth was "because you're a girl."

These lies became the rules that were supposed to protect us from some kind of problems and sufferings the grownups had experienced in their lives. But their lives are not our lives.

Without even realizing, we accepted those things as true. They embedded into our trusting young minds and became the unconscious core-beliefs that would shape us and limit us and hold us hostage for a lifetime. We tried our best to live by the rules, without knowing that some of them were never true in the first place.

If we don't unlearn the untruths, we can't become who we are meant to be. We will hide our light, whatever it is. We won't dare to live our authentic life, which is what every living soul sincerely longs for. Instinctively we knew this, even as children, but we thought we must be wrong.

The big people taught us beliefs they thought were true, and some of them might have been true, for them, at the time. But many of their beliefs likely were never true for us.

I suspected it, right from the start, didn't you? That some of them were not true? But I had to live a long time before I found out I was right. It seems like the basic soul-work for all of us is finding our untruths, unlearning, and finding what is true for us, now.

No matter what anybody told you then, or tells you now, you do have the right to be who you honestly are. The real-you is stronger, braver, great in its own way, and more wonderful than you know. If you want to know who you really are, don't ask anybody else. Don't look "out there." Don't look in the mirror. Throw out all the filters, refuse all the shoulds and can'ts. Look inside with your own heart and mind open, and believe what you see. That's who you are.

2. The Truth

When I was very young, I had faith in everything. There was nothing in my world that was likely to be anything else but wonderful. Then the big people all started teaching me to not-believe in that. They taught me how to "behave myself." They told me, "Be good and be quiet." So I did as I was told, and I slid into the shadows of things, and I became invisible. The more I grew, the more I began to notice that some of the things they taught me, just didn't feel right, but the grownups said it was supposed to be like that, so I thought it must be true.

Believing is powerful. It can make things happen or not happen. That's one of the truths nobody ever told me when I was a kid. But it's true, and it always works, like the law of gravity. So if you learn to believe that good things can't happen, for you, sure enough, they don't.

We're always believing something, whether we know it or not. All children are born believing that everything is possible, until somebody tells us it's not. What we believe is usually what we receive. That includes everyone, because that's the way this universe works.

I learned from what people said, often in spite of what they did, how life was supposed to be. But not really. What I really learned was what they thought it was supposed to be. Whatever faith and hopes they had, they taught me those. Whatever doubts and fears they had, they taught me those too. Maybe some of them knew, some of the time, that they were teaching me, so they tried to teach me things they thought would help me with life in the world. But most of them, most of the time, didn't know they were teaching, so they taught me some things they didn't even mean to, and those things stuck too.

Like all young creatures, I was rapidly absorbing everything around me, stashing it away in that spacious little brain. I was busy growing and discovering how to do things. All the rest of it I just accepted as background, without really noticing. And so I came to believe a lot of things without questioning them.

By the time I grew up, they had sunk in, and got filed away on the hard-drive of that brain, where they stayed incognito until one day a couple of decades later, I began to wonder, *Why is my life not working out so great for me? Why do I keep making the same mistakes? Getting taken advantage of, falling into the same kinds of easy traps? And then having to do the hard work of climbing out of the mess I've made?*

I began to look at those beliefs. I had to dredge them up out of the dark muddy places in my below-awareness-mind, which was a hard job in itself, and painful too. But when I did, I saw that a lot of those beliefs I accepted as a child were not really true, and had never been true – about me. When I saw that, I knew I would have to unlearn, piece by piece, the untruths that were taught to me when I was so very young, that had become hidden sub-beliefs and had shadowed my life ever since. Like: *You're not good enough unless...* and *You don't deserve it*.

It was hard. The lies had sunk so deep into the dark bottom-sand of my mind, I didn't catch on for a long time. Decades. But when I figured out that was why I kept making the same mistakes again and again, I got mad. Mad enough to demand the truth from my own self– not just the rules from everybody else. Some of rules were true and some were not. And now, each one had to be looked at in a strong light of present-time reality, and decided again, yes or no.

Was this ever true? Is it true now? If so, is it true for me? If it's not, why am I carrying it, like another brick-in-the-backpack? And then when I began to search for what was true, not for the sake of anybody else, but for me, I began to find it.

3. Looking For Grace

This week, just yesterday in fact, I asked God (again) to forgive me for every thoughtless or unintentional or unknown sin I have ever committed, and I asked Life to give me a new beginning. There are no sins I've knowingly done. (Well, except that little notebook I stole from the dime store when I was five.) I have not been unkind, dishonest, or greedy, (well maybe just for a minute sometimes.) As a kid, I really tried to be good. I admit I have entertained fears and hesitations about people and situations, and withdrawn from them, but I have resisted the urge to hold grudges, or to harbor any hatred or anger for anyone.

I know that Life can get complicated, and blame is not very useful. Sometimes what happens just happens, and we learn about life that way. My birthmother Ann was never able to love me, and I may never heal that wound, but it has faded now and I can accept it. She didn't bond with me at birth, nor could I with her in that crucial time. I was born a mottled-blue Code-3, not breathing. By necessity I was taken immediately to a cold fluorescent-lit room to be frantically resuscitated. The efforts were successful, I didn't die. But it was a terrible way to come into what must have seemed like a very terrible world.

Half a lifetime later, I was a member of an emergency medical Code 3 Team myself, and often performed advanced resuscitation procedures that were unknown at the time I was born. Out of hundreds of Code-3 resuscitations of all ages, only a few survived, because once the breathing stops, there are minutes, at best, before the heart stops and the odds get very much worse. There were many who could not be saved.

When I was born in the 1940s, I had been very fortunate to survive. A miracle they said. My life was sustained, but the cost was high. Through the same fate or act of grace that saved me, I lost my best chance to physiologically bond with the woman whose body gave birth to mine. It wasn't her fault, or mine. It was a natural consequence of circumstance, and the instinctive connection was never made. So in my first years of life, I had a birth-mother who was predisposed to be unable to love me, then the events of our lives, and perhaps some other mysteries that as a child I couldn't know, also took their toll. I didn't know this, and so I thought it must be my fault.

When I was barely a teenager, God/Life/the universe gave me a new mother who astonishingly, miraculously, loved me. It was years before I fully recognized this, because I didn't know what love looked like. I was happy being loved, I healed, and I grew strong. But even that constant love could not entirely erase the original wound, or the ones from the abusive older brother our birthmother had allowed to bully and torment me for thirteen years of my life, until the divorce changed everything.

Ahead for me there would be many other life-challenges, some dark nights of the soul, and lingering depressions. As an adult, more than once I loved and lost – to events, to a partner's addictions, or other reasons. I never got to have the love I wanted for very long. (Stop me when you hear something you never heard before and possibly experienced yourself.)

In my thirties I wondered, Is this the color of my life? All dark colors, like a bruise that can't heal? Oh, how I long for the simplest things that everybody needs: a home, a life-partner, a family or a tribe of good and lasting friends. The basic bricks and mortar of happiness.

"Love and work" Sigmund Freud said, are the two absolute essentials for a happy life. Well, I have my work, I have been loved sometimes, and I give love wherever I can, along the way. Mostly I must admit that my life has been blessed.

The reality is that all children who were unwanted in their first few years grow up feeling forever unsafe. Shelter is always a psychological priority. I've been a renter all my adult life, still rent a small apartment, and wish I could have a house, a place to live without fear of my shelter being taken away. I would love to have a life-partnership like Mother and Daddy had, my "true mother" Helen, who rescued me from the dark and lonely place where I was then. I believe I deserve that kind of love. I believe everybody deserves that. But few achieve it or receive it.

Sometimes in meditation/prayer I think, but don't say, *God do you hear me? Do you care?* This is the bedrock question for all of us who think or wonder about Life. *Whatever God is, does God care?* We mean, does God care about *me*.

We're still not too sure. Deepak Chopra says that God is Us, and We are God, and all of it is one single consciousness that is immensely bigger than our human consciousness, and we cannot know the full essence of it with just a mortal mind. We must transcend the ego-mind to a higher consciousness, which Deepak says exists, in potential, in every one of us. Mostly I believe Dr. Chopra. There have been times when I experienced other kinds or levels of consciousness. But we're still here, mortal beings in a physical world. We have to live here or die and go elsewhere.

In some ways I've already done that, died to a way of life, of everything I had known and counted on. I had to let it go, leave it behind, and begin again from nothing, it was like a death. The new life proved to be larger and richer than the one I had lost, but I didn't know that before I stepped off the precipice and took the free-fall into darkness and the unknown.

We never do. We can't. Life flows on, planets track their orbits in the cosmos, and you and I are still here, trying to understand just this one small life of our own. I feel my failures painfully, even though I know better now, that there are no mistakes, only learning places, and some of them will have pitfalls and maybe deep wounds.

So now I'm looking for another gift of grace, like the one I had at thirteen, a cosmic shift, an unexpected causeless miracle that will open a new door for me. Will it come? That's the dilemma of being human. There's so much we can never know, and we want to know, so bad. But if we knew it all, there would be no more to discover, and no reason to stay.

4. No Mistakes

I got up early, made coffee, and sat down in my reading/thinking corner near the stove. Idly I pulled out a book from the bookshelf, one I'd been reading several years ago and then had put aside. When I flipped it open, I was surprised to find a very old letter folded inside. I had placed it there for a bookmark, as I often do with such things. It was a birthday letter, the last one from someone I had loved for seven years.

It was dated fourteen years after our life together had ended. For all of those years, until I moved from Berkeley and left no forwarding address, he had written me letters once a year to wish me love and a happy birthday. They were sweet and simple and sincere. I didn't save them, I couldn't. They were as heartbreaking as they were beautiful, and my mind fiercely fought to push away the feelings of loss and regret. I had kept this one, even though it was deeply painful, because I knew it would be the last one. I could not bring myself to throw it out. Now as I realized what it was, even before I opened it, my eyes flooded with tears.

Why had the letter surfaced again? And why now? Maybe I needed to be reminded that I had once been loved, truly and deeply. Whatever the reason, the letter set me to thinking about how life takes us where it will, not where we want to go. Sometimes the soul has another plan.

He was my life-partner for seven years, and though we had never married, we were truly together, a part of each other. He was the polar opposite of the man I did marry when I was too young to know any better. Instead he was aways kind, always thoughtful, always there for me. He smiled and shook his head, called me his "complicated lady." He knew he would probably never entirely understand me, but he didn't need that. He loved me "as-is." It was the kind of love we all dare to hope for.

When it ended I knew there would never be another love like that for me, never another soul who could touch my soul like that. But I also knew, even through the blinding pain, that this part of my life was gone, there was no way to get it back.

While we were together, we loved each other completely, and for the first time in my life I knew for sure that I was loved. But life swept us into different directions that tore us apart profoundly, like tearing the wings from a butterfly. Wings don't grow back. You have to find another way to fly, and there may not be a way.

Life hurts sometimes. But if we are lucky enough or blessed by grace enough to have a perfect moment, a perfect year, or a season of love, we find ourselves in a wonderful place and we want to stay. But we can't stay, anywhere in this life. That's not the way it works. Life itself is movement and change.

I think I could have stayed in love with him forever, but life had other plans for me, and for him too. There was more to do, and much more to learn. Our paths diverged and we could only follow them, even if into darkness for a while before there could be light again. We could only follow where life was taking us, and this is true for everyone. You can only go, or not go, where your life leads you. To not-follow would be death-in-life, incarceration of the Spirit, and both are impossible. Life will find a way out.

In Mother and Daddy, Helen and George, I witnessed a near-perfect love. Once life brought them together, they loved and cherished each other for the rest of their lives. Helen rescued me and my brother, teenage kids she knew were troubled ones. That could not have been easy, and it was a big risk that there could be enough love in this put-together family to pull it off, but she did. She and Daddy faced some tough challenges, but from the start, they took on everything in life together.

Before they found each other, each of them had suffered some painful wounds of failure and loss in their first marriage, as I would do also. Each of them must have gone through times when they cried alone and hid the hurt so no one would see, just like I did. But once they were brought together, not really by chance but by some inexplicable movement of cosmic grace, a new kind of life opened up for them, a new unimagined adventure, and a love that would hold strong for nearly five decades, and then forever.

"Nothing happens by chance," says the book, A Course In Miracles. "Everything that happens, comes for a reason." Life is about learning, and we are here in this place to learn and to grow our souls. I believe that.

I traveled a long long way to discover this simple truth, even though it was one that my grandmother told me when I was six or seven. My Granny was wise. I was too young to understand at the time, but she was right. Nothing that happens is a mistake. Nothing we do with earnest intention can be wrong.

She said, *"There are really no mistakes, as long as you are sincere. They are just places to learn. Do the best you can, and that will be enough."*

And she said, "One choice takes you here, and one choice takes you there, but whatever you choose takes you somewhere, and then you can choose again."

– Jessie B. Vaughn, 1876-1952

5. How You See It

When you try to do something and you fail, that seems to suggest that you can't do it. Suggest, but not prove. This is where you have to decide, and choose between either letting it go or trying harder. If you try again and you fail again, the suggestion gets stronger, so the determination must get stronger too, or there's also the option to let go of that endeavor, and move on.

Does that make you a quitter? Or a failure? This too is your choice. Giving up too soon or too often is not a strength, and it's not a disgrace either, but the price you pay is, you never give yourself a fighting chance.

Everything that happens in life is open to interpretation, and ultimately the only interpretation, opinion, or belief that really matters is yours, because that is the only one that actually has any true power or influence on your life.

The children's rhyme "sticks and stones may break my bones but words can never hurt me" is not quite true, words can hurt a lot. But they cannot conquer you unless you choose to let them. You always have the choice: are you going to let somebody else, out there, set your course in life? Will you choose to let their opinion change your inner knowing that you are more than they can see? Are you doing that now?

Once in a conversation, a firefighter friend told me "You can do it if you set your mind to it." I wanted fiercely to become a firefighter, but as a woman, five-foot-six and 112 pounds, the odds against it were enormous. Three years of pumping iron, running bleachers with a backpack full of sand, 30-mile bike rides, and several failed firefighter physical agility tests later, finally one day I didn't fail. I passed that one, and then I passed some more. Eventually I did become a firefighter, then an officer. Though I started late, I served eight years as an active duty Firefighter and Emergency Medical first-responder, and put in a surprisingly good performance record. My friend was right.

Since then, whenever I've had to set a difficult goal and it's something that my heart wants so much I can't bear it, I know I've got to try. I know I may not get it the first time, and I may not get it at all, and failures will be crushingly demeaning, but I've got to try. Some things don't come easy. I know that. And most of the best things don't.

I've been a fool a few times, and looked like a fool many times, but I wouldn't trade the adventure or a single bruising rock in the road I stumbled over in that path, for anything else in this world.

Here's a truth: If you pay attention, you can learn more from failing than from succeeding. If you start out not strong enough, you have to learn how to get strong, and then that learning and confidence will be there for you in everything else you do. The experience of failure is always painful and humbling, and yet it's also the ultimate challenge to your inner strength. To have failed before you succeed creates opportunities to develop endurance, character, courage, and spiritual strength.

A failure is one experience that can come between you and success, one rock in the road. Everything depends on how you choose to see it. Life is wide open to any unlimited number of interpretations. The one that matters most, is yours.

Ravi Shankar said: "Life is like a river. The river does not stop because there is a stone"

6. Courage and Faith

The basic laws of life are always working, even if we are totally unaware: "What we believe is what we receive," also called "the Law of Attraction," is lesson #1 of the New Thought faiths and the New Paradigm. This Truth Principle is the winner's edge, as well as the loser's self-defeating curse, because we can only be that which we are willing to dare to believe we can be.

Another Law of the universe, Karma, in the simplest terms is "What you give is what you get." Sooner or later, life unfailingly returns to us, in like kind, whatever we have put out into the lifestream. These truths are ancient, so since we are all the same creatures more or less, why do some of us do only just-okay, (or not) and others do magnificent things?

It looks like, in almost every aspect of this life on earth, courage becomes the difference-maker. That, along with a rock-solid commitment to hold onto our "foolish" faith, sets every seemingly-impossible dream into forward-motion.

"Nothing is impossible if you have faith." Jesus said, among other radical ideas that got him in trouble for telling the truth. That's what he and other great teachers and messengers came here to tell us about– the power of faith. Even a little faith. (If you want to move mountains however, I recommend more than a little.) The greater the faith, the better the outcome. But faith is not easy. It requires courage. If your heart and soul truly passionately desire something "impossible," don't play the odds. Go for it, all out.

Impossible is just a word until proven otherwise. I've done a few "impossible" things. that turned out to be not impossible, just really really hard. If you can even let yourself believe you might, and you're willing to do the work, all bets are off. The power of the universe gets behind that. If you're willing to do the work, and you dare to believe you can do it, you will.

7. Writing From Within

There are times when I'm writing and I realize *I'm not* writing it, I'm just writing it down. I'm getting the message, receiving it. Not making it up, just passing it on.

I started to write a memoir but it has become an epistle of faith. When I look back across my history and the history of my family, I see patterns and meaning that I never saw at the time it was happening. There was purpose in all of it. Whatever happens in Life with a capital "L" we are led by something greater than we know.

This book is emerging not from my outer, ego-world mind-view, but more as if spoken from some inner voice, uncontrived and unplanned. Whatever comes to me that rings true, I write it down. I know that *if it has value, it will stay, and everything else eventually will fall away.* Things take care of themselves. All my poetry came this way, gifts of grace, never the product of effort, or skill. It comes, and I write it down. I trust the soundless voice that speaks, more than I trust my own limited intellect.

In my twenties as an artist and a fledgling poet, I said once in a moment of inspiration, "Lord, make me your instrument." Maybe God will finally do that, or maybe He was the one that placed that idea there to begin with.

My basic prayer hasn't changed much, even as I've made my mistakes, learned, and relearned. By myself I can do little of real significance, but when I'm driven to the page by that unnamed silent voice, something clear and true flows out into the light of ordinary day. In that moment, the ordinariness, the stories, the simple truths of life, take on a different energy that somehow transcends their material substance. What's written becomes more than the words.

I write them down as fast as I can. And then, thunder-struck I read them, to see what they will say.

8. Snapshot

There's a little photograph I keep on my refrigerator door, of three women sitting in a porch swing on the plain wooden porch of a farmhouse somewhere in rural Illinois. The women pose for the Kodak camera with their hands folded neatly in their laps.

The house is small, made of clapboard neatly painted white. It's summer. Emerald green fields of corn stretch out behind the house and seem to go all the way to the horizon. At the front of the house, two windows face the road, plain and functional, with no curtains. The porch shade is enough to keep out the midday sun, and there are no neighbors near enough to look in.

It's Sunday after church, and the women are my mother and my two sisters. They have traveled all the way from Dallas Texas to Bloomington Illinois for Mother's 50th high school reunion. This house is a place where Mother lived as a young girl a long time ago, and the current residents have welcomed her to the old homestead and invited all of them to stay for dinner. In this small snapshot I can see through time, to the past generations of strong farm women, practical, hard-working and generous. I love this little picture for its sweetness, its honesty and simplicity.

Mother has left us now, gone from this earth to a higher calling. Both of my sisters still live in Texas and have grown children. My own path has taken me from Texas to the East Coast, to the Midwest, and finally to the West Coast of Northern California where I call home, a long long way from both Texas and Illinois.

I take the picture down from its magnet on the fridge door. I hold it in my hand for a moment. I hold these women in my heart forever.

9. We Are Revealed

In David White's book, *The Heart Aroused,* he writes about "authentic voice," and he says: "Whether or not we tried to tell the truth, in the very act of speech, no matter what we say, we are revealed." I notice that in my reading notes I had written, just below the quotation, "I know this. I have experienced it."

It's true. When someone lies to me, I usually know it, and I know that no matter what words they are saying, what they are really telling me is:

"I am a liar. I am lying to you now, I have lied before and I will lie again, because this is the way I "do business." It's my choice; it works for me. This is who I am, and I am convinced that I'm right, and I'm better and smarter than you."

Quietly I smile at the lie, because what I find interesting is that these people don't even realize what they are showing about themselves. They think everyone else is too dumb to notice. We're not. Most people know, almost by a sixth sense or a gut-feeling when someone is lying to them. (My granny always knew.) We tend to give everyone "the benefit of the doubt" in case we're mistaken, but more often than not, sooner or later it turns out that our instinct or intuition was correct.

We also know that anyone who lies once will lie again, and when next we engage those persons, we are unlikely to waste our trust on them, and a space opens up between us.

It is this space, not the lie itself, that is the tragic cost.

10. FYI, I Love You

One of the few regrets in my life has been that I spent so many years not saying I love you to people I loved. Some of them have left this world now, and even though I tell them in my evening meditations and prayers, I no longer have the opportunity to tell them face-to-face.

This is a habit that so many of us have – holding back and not expressing the good things we think and feel about each other. There are different reasons. Mine was that I was embarrassed, and my family had not been outwardly affectionate when I was young. For many of us it just seems easier, or safer, but it has a cost. Not saying I love you, not saying I'm proud of you, not saying I respect you for who you are, has a cost because life is short and unpredictable. Once the moment passes, we may never get that opportunity again, and never know how much it might have meant to someone.

Now I just go ahead and tell people. What a radical idea! No big deal, not the romantic I-love-you, but just the friendship I-love-you, the Mom, Dad, sister, brother I-love-you. I believe it's good to tell people who probably already know we love them, or ought to know. But do they know for sure? It might actually matter to them more than we thought.

I always smile at strangers that pass me on the sidewalk. A stranger's smile saved my life once. Smiles cost nothing at all, you can give away zillions of them every day. Try it. You'll never regret a single one.

11. The Darkness / Let It Be

After most of a lifetime of trying to be better than I am, stronger than I am, refusing to ever admit defeat, I finally said to myself one night, right out loud, "Too bad! This is what I am. I'm doing the best I can. If it's not enough for you, then walk on by!"

Nobody was there at the time.

Then I cried a whole lot of crocodile tears and I decided to start treating myself like a friend instead of a snarky self-critic. That wasn't working so well for me anyway. Maybe I read it in a book, I don't know, but I started letting myself feel what I was feeling, instead of pretending everything was fine when it wasn't, instead of feeling like I must never weaken even in my own secret thoughts, or that would mean I failed.

I didn't fail just because I didn't do it this time! Or I didn't do it like somebody else did it! And if I did it better this time than the last time, dammit, I deserve credit!

Well, I didn't do anything crazy in public, but I started giving myself the right to be whoever I was on any given day. Some days I was pretty cool, other days I stumbled over my words and my own feet like a stupid fool. I allowed that.

When times got really rocky, I hid someplace and let myself cycle through whatever emotions came, including the ones that hurt, and the ugly ones I knew were unworthy of the person I wanted to be, who was the greater truth of me.

In my life, there have been times when sorrow, jealousy, righteous resentment, and a few times even rage have taken hold of me, feelings I didn't dare to admit, let alone express. Cramming them down into the dark boggy bottom of my mind did not extinguish the "un-noble" feelings. Instead it gave them the perfect place to wretchedly squirm and fester and thrive. That did not feel good, and it did not heal them.

After decades of fighting against my unworthy emotions, I

have come to the acceptance of the reality of my human state:

I am imperfect. Tons of energy and huge parts of me have been wasted battling this truth. I am only a traveler here, unwise but teachable, and we have all come here to learn.

It's true that I've got some attributes I wish I didn't have. They provide me with learning opportunities to become less of what I don't want to be, and more of what I know I can be.

The truest and best parts of me (and you) have never been sullied or changed by the upstart flashes of our worst parts. When I remind myself of this, it sets my feet on solid ground again, and I know that in this moment's storm of emotions I am not wrong, just floundering, stumbling, learning. I can and will ride it out, and return to the essence of me that is really who I want to be.

When I need to rage for a while, I let myself. I give myself a private rant or pity-party, whichever is needed, and I set a time limit. Then when it's done, I forgive myself for it, and start over. I make myself do this without holding onto any residue of shame or guilt. Plain-old forgiveness releases me and everyone else from the trap of whatever it was. The ugliness gets vented and disintegrates into the nothingness from which it came.

If I dissolve into pathetic wimpy tears for a while, I let myself. When my mini-drama of spirit, dark moment of the soul has expressed itself and passed on, I comfort myself. I forgive and release all feelings of shame or weakness, the things I used to punish myself for.

In private I accept, forgive, and pledge to love this part of me too, just as I would forgive and love a little child who never really meant any harm, but she just didn't know any better, and she has not learned everything yet.

It's getting easier to love who I am. I'm kinder and more forgiving to everybody else too. When bad feelings come, I know how to handle them, and they do not handle me. In a private place I let the feelings come, *and then I let them go.*

I feel better, and when I go back to the business of my life, sure enough, *I do better.*

12. Mothers

It could be said that I've had two mothers in my life. Of those two, the first one, my biological mother, I remember only partially, and with uncertainty, and I've only recently grown strong enough to call her by any m-name. I call her very respectfully "my birthmother Ann." When I was with her, she was called Mama.

My birthmother was not able to love me the way I needed and probably deserved to be loved, and she loved my brother Tommy more than was healthy for him or for herself. I never really knew her. That was my first and deepest wound: that she had not wanted to know me.

My true Mother wanted me, although I didn't understand why until I grew up. I was thirteen when she fell in love with my dad, and life and the legal system gave me to her. Mother, Helen, loved me astonishingly, even though I had no reason to deserve it at all. She was a person who loved to love. It was her nature. I was an awkward shy half-feral stray, and she, like a rescuing angel in a movie too good to be true, brought me home and loved me.

Some people would say I had a terrible mother until then. It was true enough in some ways, but it wasn't all her fault. When I was eleven, her marriage was falling apart, and alcoholism was dragging her down. She sank deeper and faster. I could feel it, but I couldn't understand it, or the divorce, or any of that. I just knew I felt bad, I thought it was somehow my fault. I knew she was unhappy, but I didn't know how to help her, and my brother didn't either. Looking back, I believe she turned to alcohol the way so many people do, to escape from her pain.

"Unfit mother" they said in the custody court, but she was alone and broke with two kids to feed, then she fell down drunk and broke her arm and lost her waitress job. In the first two years after the divorce, the three of us, she and my brother and I, kept having to move. Three times in two years, always to smaller and shabbier apartments. We ended up in an abandoned boarded-up house at the back of a windblown vacant lot. I called it the haunted house. It was winter and there was only one small open-flame gas heater. Some of the windows were broken out and the wind howled through the boards, and the cold seeped over the casements and flowed into the house like an icy stream. After we moved to the boarded-up house with no address, I didn't know where Daddy lived, and I was afraid he wouldn't be able to find me, but he did.

    Some weekends he took me to see my best girlfriends in the old neighborhood, or to a movie, and then to meet Helen and play with her daughters Mary and Martha. I was very shy, but she respected that. She let me help her with the wonderful hot meals she made for all of us to eat when Daddy came in the evening after work. Tommy didn't come. He was off somewhere with this friends, stealing cars and other mostly show-off crimes of teenage rebellion.

    It was great to go to Helen's house and eat hot food. It was so good! And there was so much of it! Then Daddy had to bring me back to where Mama and Tommy and I lived in the cold empty house. Daddy didn't know that other times I stole Twinkies and meat from the Safeway store, and fruit and vegetables from the baskets of wilted produce they set out in back on the loading dock for the garbage truck, because there wasn't any food in the house, and
I was too ashamed to tell him.

    October came, when I had just started junior high school. There was a freezing rain the night before, and when I left the house to go to school the next morning, I went skittering down the sheet-ice on the sidewalk to the street. I saw Daddy's old green Desoto parked there, and he and Helen were in it. They called to me, so I got in the car. They asked if they could come into the house. No one was there, so I said, "Okay, I guess." I took them in through the back door hidden among the weeds.

When Helen saw the cold dark dusty house and the empty refrigerator, she was upset, and I thought I might be in trouble. She and Daddy stood together talking very quietly. I couldn't hear what they said, but she had tears in the corners of her clear blue eyes.

They packed my clothes and belongings in a paper grocery bag and they kidnapped me. They broke the law, and I'm not saying that was okay, but in total surprise and bafflement, I did not resist. In less than an hour I was transferred to a new school, I had a unimaginable new life, and a beautiful new mother.

She wanted me, and she wanted to know me. She loved to do things for me. She taught me things, like how to make baking powder biscuits from scratch that were like big delicious clouds of wonderfulness. How to sew, how to look nice and to walk proud. She taught me modest dignity and a little bit of personal style. I'm not sure when I first began to call her Mother, but it was soon, and it lasted forever.

She had brought me out of that lonely life like a miracle of the sheer grace of God, and yet she never would have even met me except that by some mysterious link in the cogs and wheels of the universe, she met my dad and they fell in love. It was a love so deep, so cherished and so beautiful that it lasted the rest of their lives. They got married and filed for legal custody of my brother and me.

It was Helen, my true mother, who lifted me up out of the grim desolation of a life with no hope of a future. When she saw how it was for me, she couldn't leave me there, not for another day, not for another minute, and all of a sudden I had won the cosmic lottery. I got the most generous, kind, smart, strong, loving mother on earth, and incredibly, she wanted me. She loved me from the start, and until the very last moment of her life. She and Daddy would love each other forever, and beyond.

She encouraged my brother and me to keep in touch with our birthmother and she arranged visits for us. But seeing her again was confusing and almost unbearable for us, and for her I'm sure much worse. She must have felt ashamed, defeated, lost and sad. After the first visit, my brother never went back. I did, but in a few years I went off to college and my life became full of wonderful other things.

The next time I saw her was my wedding day. Mother had sent her an announcement out of respect. No one thought she would come, but she did. That took some courage. I didn't see her at the wedding, but there she was at the reception. So much was happening that I didn't really speak with her or she with me, but she was clean and sober, she looked healthy, and prettier than I had ever seen her.

Then the last time I saw her was after my divorce. She got on a plane for the first time in her life and flew to Minneapolis to see me. I didn't know what I would say or do, but I couldn't refuse.

I didn't know what she had hoped for, but there was no miracle reunion. We were strangers, and the encounter tore open old wounds that I'd hidden from myself all those years. It was painful to even talk. We both tried, but there could not be any reunion where there had never really been a union in the first place.

After she left, we wrote letters as adult friends for the next ten years, until she died. Most of what I know of her, I learned from those letters. She died in Dallas where my brother still lived. He had refused to speak to her for forty years. He buried her the day before I could get there from California.

My parents divorce had been a mystery to me as a child. Now, I know that Life can be complicated, not easily analyzed, and often wrongly judged. Ann was a decent woman who had wounds of her own. I think she believed she didn't deserve better, and she taught me that I didn't either. It wasn't true, about either of us. She never meant to hurt me, or anyone.

In my true Mother's steadfast love, my wounds healed, and I grew strong. But even that love couldn't entirely erase the scars. I am no longer ashamed of them, but some days are harder than others. I wish I could have done more for my biological mother, but I know that we both did all we were able to do. The truth is, everyone has wounds. My catharsis has been to write a book, the memoir of my stumbling path, healing from the inside out.

I wish healing for you too, and for all of us in the family of humanity. Not one of us is without wounds and scars and flaws. Please accept, respect, and love this part of yourself, as I do in myself, and in you.

13. How To Write The Hard Stuff

Some things are hard to write, especially when you've made a commitment to telling the truth. In most families, there's a lot to forgive. Forgiving my birthmother was natural, and though it was painful and took a few decades, it was always inevitable. Life would teach me that we are all bound to make mistakes, and we all do mostly the best we can. She got caught up in the downward spiraling trap of alcohol, like millions of other decent people also did. There was nothing really that needed to be forgiven. She had done the best she could.

My brother was different. He took pleasure in tormenting me physically and psychologically throughout our childhood. It was he who taught me that victim/martyr was supposed to be my role in life. In the memoir, even though I tried to be as discreetly kind as possible, he still comes off as the devious, selfish, controlling bully that in fact he was.

Part of the unexpected epiphany of writing the memoir was my own overcoming of the still-lingering fears and feelings of low self-worth and victimization that my brother had taught me when we were children. These self-destructive false beliefs had followed me into my failed marriage and beyond. They were subconscious lies, hidden from my awareness, and so I would suffer blindly much longer than I should have. Most people would say I had a lot to forgive.

Forgiveness is often an underlying theme of memoirs, because it's one of the things every life must come to terms with in some degree. Writing the book, I chose to skim over the worst things about my brother, but I didn't try to make him something he wasn't. And there were other unhealed wounds because of how our birthmother allowed him to abuse me as he did, which I could not understand, and that hurt me even more. The reasons were always there, but I never saw them until I wrote the book, and then in the last chapter, they revealed themselves to me and to my readers at the same time.

Memoir is the most personal kind of writing. I will never advise anyone about how they should do it, except maybe to recommend that you simply throw all caution and politeness out the window and be as honest and emotionally courageous as you possibly can, in your first drafts.

Blow it all out there. Surprise and horrify yourself with how ugly some of the truth is, and how ravaging some of your unspoken feelings are. Later you can change or modify any of it as much as you want or need to do, but getting that first raw truth on paper will reveal to you so much about yourself, it will give intense life-force to your writing, and it will truly help you heal a great many things in the long run.

Truth is the essence and life-blood of memoir. If you're going to write a memoir, don't skimp on your own agonizing honesty in it. That's what rewrites are for. Right now, allow yourself the absolute blameless entitlement to feel anything you feel, even if it's not beautiful. Some of it will be uglier than you ever knew.

Even if you're not writing anything whatsoever, and maybe you're just trying to understand your life, *same thing.* Tell the truth, write it down in your journal. Admit everything you have ever been ashamed of, and then take another look at it, one piece at a time. Do this with intentional compassion, especially for yourself. Take as long as you need.

I promise you, you will see a lot of things differently, more truly and more kindly this time. The understanding of yourself that this brings at the deepest level will move you, whether gently or excruciatingly, toward a clearer and truer understanding of everything.

14. Into The Light

So many of us live our lives invisibly, floating like a dust mote in the air, unseen until the light catches it drifting through a sunshaft, golden for a moment, then gone again.

I've noticed lately that life is short, sometimes shorter than we expect, so I say, spend as much of it as you can in the sunshaft. Be willing to be seen. Step into the light and let life shine on you. It's actually not as scary as you think.

Try something different. Do something more. Wear your heart on your sleeve. Step out of the shadows and onto the water. Miracles happen every day, but it's like my granny said "You've got to walk out under the sky and let the blessings fall on you. They're not going to come and look for you hiding under the bed."

We don't exactly hide under the bed, except figuratively speaking, but the trending technology has removed many of the necessities of ever having to look at each other, or speak to each other face to face. This is not really a good thing.

Consider getting a bit old-fashioned now and then. Openly care about somebody, and don't worry if they know it. Maybe even, tell them you care. What a radical idea!

Try it. You might like it. What have you got to lose? Except a little loneliness? And really you don't need that anyway. Love is better. Friends are better. Neighbors are better. Go ahead, try it. I dare you.

15. The Edge Of Reality

The New Thought faiths, based as they are on the study of many ancient faiths, considered, integrated and merged, reveal that "It's all God" and "God is all there is." This means that all of Life, and each of us, is actually an embodiment and Expression of God. It means we are cut from the same infinite cloth, and one with all that is. Jesus and others have said, "God is within."

But wait a minute– if I accept that, and if I believe that I am, myself, an embodiment and Expression of God, then does that mean there is no God "out there?" No Grandfather-God to turn to? No God to thank? No God to show up like a knight in armor to rescue me from the messes I make in my life? If there is only an in-here God and no more out-there God, where is my help? Are we on our own in the cosmos?

That seemed to me like the loneliest thing that can ever be experienced, and to be honest, it scared me. For me, and I think for a whole lot of human beings, "oneness with God" sounds like a big responsibility, and almost seems like an abandonment.

So I'm still holding on, a little bit, to the version of God from my childhood that I still need– somebody to talk to when things get too rough or too lonely or too hard. I have read, and I believe this, that God makes Himself available to all of us, each in the way that we can personally understand.

Lately things have been going strangely wrong around me. I have been all ferklempt and scared a lot. Last night at twilight I prayed, as I usually do, but this time it was not my usual silent meditation and softly-spoken prayer. It was one of those Jacob-wrestling-with-the-angel prayers where you rant at the evening sky like a lunatic. At one point I broke down in a flood of tears and I said to God out loud, "It's just too big!" (my soul's assignment, the book.) "It's so much bigger than I am. You've got to help me do it! You've GOT TO help me!"

There have been a few times in my life when the skies opened up. Not this time. There was no new epiphany, no bush bursting into flames, and no holy revelation. There was no stunning shift in consciousness, only the calm, dark, absolute, silence. Sometimes it's hard not to worry if maybe God is mad at me.

But I know that the image of some rewarding-and-punishing or loving-and-abandoning Super-Parent-God isn't real. It's something we human beings made up, one of the many versions of God we've created in order to help ourselves understand. But these versions of God can be dangerous, because they are as real as we make them, and in this life, what we believe, we receive.

The gentle sheltering God I knew as a child still exists, those times when I can become a child again and look at life with a child's faith and trust.

But how can I do that now, God? Now that I know too much? Now that I've seen what life can do? The world is in turmoil, people are suffering who shouldn't have to suffer, and people I've loved have passed away. There is always too much work to do, I can't do it and yet I must. And I fear and dread the faster and faster passing of time ...

And thus I howled at the Almighty in the night sky.

But at the end of my raging, whining prayer, there was only the peace and silence of darkness.

I felt foolish, but I felt better. I had in effect, thrown a tantrum, and yet God had not struck me down with a lightning bolt for being bad. (Even though I knew I was bad, and I still did it anyway, much like a 2-year old.) Then in the aftermath, in the lovely peace and stillness, I remembered the first time I had done this – talked out loud at God like He was in the room. It was twilight then too.

And next my mind wandered to a time decades ago when I

was in college. We were all artists and philosophers then, and there was a saying, "There is a thin line between genius and insanity." A close friend once confided in me that he believed twilight was the time when the mind was at its thinnest and weakest point, and in that brief hour, there was a danger of slipping through to the other side of reality, and possibly not being able to come back. That scared me a little, but I was young and happy so I soon forgot about it.

It was about five years later when my first out-loud-prayer happened. It wasn't scary, in fact, I was just *thinking a prayer,* a regular ordinary kind of one, and then I sort-of drifted into the prayer itself. I didn't notice at first that I was talking, calmly at normal volume and entirely spontaneously, and then suddenly I heard myself talking to somebody all by myself in an empty room.

A flash of fear shot through me that made my scalp tingle, and I wondered for a second or two if maybe I had lost my mind. Shocked, I stopped.

I listened carefully to the silence.

Nothing happened. I had not lost my mind, and I didn't get captured by any evil forces from the other side of The Veil. But something had changed. Something in me had gently shifted and broken through to a different level.

Life has rolled on. Now I guess God has gotten used to this, along with my many other oddities. Whatever I bring to Him now, apparently He has heard worse. And He doesn't complain about the noise.

16. Rain Thoughts

The strangest things go running through my mind on rainy afternoons like this, when the sky is the color of slate, so gloomy that it's almost dark, and a chilly drizzle is dripping from the roof-eaves outside the window. I drift away, and before I even know it, I have slipped into time-traveling.

Rainy days are not good for much except making love or taking naps. Neither is on my agenda today. What happened to spring? I don't know. Just a flicker of sunlight and then the rains came back again.

Rainy days put my mind into a vaporous state, and I start remembering sad things, or people I've known and cared about who went away, or died. Same thing really.

It's impossible to understand life or God. I've tried, but I can't even understand my own self, never mind anything as big and profound as God. But I've learned to just go ahead, even when I can't see where I'm going, even if sometimes I'm scared. Because if I didn't do that, I wouldn't go-ahead much at all, since most of the time I can't see where I'm going and some of the times when I thought I could, it turned out that I was going in the wrong direction anyway.

Feeling melancholy today. Funny word. Wait, I'll look it up. "Sorrowful, dismal, mournful, lugubrious, despondent, forlorn, disconsolate, morose . . . "

No, that's not it, maybe "nostalgic." I'll look up that one: "yearning, longing, pensive, reflective, contemplative." Yes, more like that. I feel like an unwound clock. This morning I was full of energy, and then the darkness flowed into my day and smothered my spark under these woolly gray clouds.

On days like this, I look at my life, and it looks like a follow-the-dots puzzle. Being abandoned, being rescued, falling in and out of love. Someday when most of the wildly scattered dots are connected, will they make a picture? Will the picture make sense?

My memory unaccountably whirls back to college again.

Oh, the taken-for-granted joys, each day an adventure! Being with other art students and peers, and we were all so young and lovely and spiritually bullet-proof.

What wonderful days those were! I don't remember ever worrying about anything– not even midterm exams. I was in love with life, and art, and beautiful moments, and every part of me was intensely alive. Back then I think we all felt everything more, from happiness to heartbreak, to the slightest breeze on our skin. We art majors were different from the rest. We were not mere students, but seekers, explorers, discoverers. We grew like flowering vines in every direction at once, blossoming and dropping careless beauty randomly all along our way.

Funny how such odd things pop into your mind like this, when the rain stops time.

College for me ended one semester short of graduation. I married another artist and moved to the East Coast to support him through graduate school at Yale, working a soul-numbing clerical job at the Telephone Company. Women, wives, did that then. My young husband wasn't a bad person, he was just thoughtless, spoiled by his single-mom who loved him too much. She was wonderful to me too. He was clueless and thoughtless. He was sexually demanding and totally ungiving in that way. He didn't know how, and I didn't either. It wasn't personal. It didn't involve me at all, just my body that he owned. I didn't know that I deserved better.

In the beginning when we met, he was talented, smart, and funny and we were friends. He was the classic temperamental artist. He was intense. He stood out. I was so young and naive, I thought he was some kind of wonderful. Yes, he was self-centered, well who wasn't, then? But he had a tender spirit.

He was the one who showed me that rainy days could be beautiful, one morning in college when we looked out the window of his little basement apartment in Austin at the raindrops glittering on each bitter-green blade of grass and clover leaf. It was a high narrow horizontal window, just about shoulder-height in the little basement room, but level with the ground outside, the grass, and the misty air. The spring rain was so delicate, it was magical. I had never seen the rain as anything so lovely before.

It was that part of him, the part that shared with me the intimacy of the rain, his gentleness, his tenderness, that I fell in love with. But he never gave me that again.

I've known other beautiful rains since then, and eventually I would have my share of beautiful lovers too. I got over the pain of the bad beginning I'd had in my marriage, but the inner scars took longer to heal. There would be lots of pretty young men, but no matter how sweet they were, I did not allow them into my heart. It was five years before I dared to take the risk of loving again. But this time, *I was loved,* and all the years before, faded away.

I had been a naive virgin when I met the brash and equally naive young man I married when we were both too young to know any better. He didn't know that sex should be personal, and I didn't know that sex could be, and should be, something that felt good, even wonderful,. I didn't know that I had a right to say yes or no. By the the time I learned those things, and I knew that I deserved them, he was thousands of miles behind me.

I still think of him once in a while, on a rainy day like this, and wonder if he's happy, or if he's even still alive. He was an alcoholic and suffered from depressions and fits of rage, and always carried a deep unresolved sadness about his father's suicide when he was 16.

Oh yes, we all have a story.

God bless you Jim, maybe I'll see you in heaven. You won't recognize me. I've changed.

17. Query Letters and Cowboy Boots

As I write the memoir, I'm putting together the necessary query letter to send to my potential agents and publishers. This is the first level of approach and sales-pitch in the quest to get published. My publisher will want to know "Who will read this book?" (In other words, Who will *buy* his book.) This book will likely be catalogued as a "women's" book, but really, almost everyone must struggle to fit Who We Are into What The World Expects or demands of us. Truth be told, that includes most of humanity.

We spend the first few decades of our lives trying to understand who we are, and even if we succeed, we will still have to find the courage to dare to be that. The hardest obstacles are the deeply-embedded untruths we were taught about ourselves when we were children, told to us by people who should have loved us but didn't, or people who did love us, and told us those things because they thought they were protecting us from life.

In the memoir, the story opens with a skinny little girl running through the neighborhood fantasizing that she's a race-horse. She likes climbing trees and roofs, splashing through rain puddles, running and leaping over hedges and fences. She adores horses and fire engines, but she gets repeatedly told by the big people "You can't do that..." "you can't have that..." and " you can't be that..." (every single thing she loves) "...because you're a girl." What's worse, there is always the powerful unspoken mandate: "You shouldn't want those things."

"Who says?!" She demands, but to no avail. She asks, "Why not?" and gets no reasonable answer. "Those things are for boys," they say. What she hears clearly is: What you want and who you are is not okay.

It was a big fat lie, and somewhere in every child's heart

we all knew this, but what could we do? We were just a kid. We depended on the big people to tell us what life was supposed to be, and we believed them. Some of what they told us wasn't true, but the same untruths had been told to them, and passed along for generations.

When we were so young, so vulnerable and trusting, and just beginning to learn what life was supposed to be, most of us got informed either by words or actions, "You shouldn't be who you are, you should be something else." (Something better, smarter, prettier, stronger, more like what they want than what we are.) If you're a boy, you've got to like cars and guns and baseball, not art or music or poetry. Girls must like dolls, dresses and tea-sets, not mud, horses and fire engines.

I remember with crystal clarity the day my brother got cowboy boots. Daddy brought them home for him. I had seen cowboy movies, and I was crazy about horses, boots and spurs and everything-cowboy, so I got all excited and asked, "Ooooh! Do I get some cowboy boots too?"

My parents chuckled, "Oh no honey, cowboy boots are for boys. You can have some pretty ballet slippers..."

I think I was three years old then.

"Ballet slippers? No! *Who wants THAT?!*" And I begged for cowboy boots too. It didn't do any good. Even now I can still feel the ache and sting of being so terribly wronged and cheated. I pleaded in my own defense, "I can't help it if I was born a girl! I didn't get to choose!"

Later I would become a closet-tomboy. At home I was quiet and obedient, but I sneaked out to climb trees and roofs and fire-escapes and run around the neighborhood imagining myself as something beautiful: a fast, sleek, marvelous racehorse. And so I grew up. I didn't want to, but I learned to "act like a lady" and I followed the rules.

Seven-eights of the way through college, I married a bright

hopeful art student like myself, gave up my beautiful joyful life and went to work at the Telephone Company to put my husband through graduate school. I was a good wife. He never noticed.

He went to school and I went to work. After work I cooked dinner while he watched Rocky and Bullwinkle on TV. When dinner was ready, he brought the little TV and set it on the table. If I asked, "How was your day?" He said, "I don't feel like talking. I just need to relax." So I let him.

After dinner I was left with the dishes while he went to a favorite student pub for frosty mugs of cold beer and conversation with other bright minds like his own. At closing time he stumbled home, helped himself to my body without comment, then turned over and went instantly to sleep. I cried a little, then I went to sleep too. I had to get up early and go to work.

Every week I signed over my paycheck for him to deposit in his checking account. At the rare student and faculty functions he he took me to, he introduced me as "the wife." I spent the loneliest four and a half years of my life like that, until I realized. *I have no Life, and I have no Self.*

I was living invisible in his shadow. Before we married, I had been an artist too, like him. But whoever I was before had been sacrificed and lost somewhere. It was not his fault, or mine. We both played the roles we had been brought up to play.

Even though it was empty, leaving that life was shattering. It was not just a failure, it was a death, the end of a life that had failed. *The end of a lie* I tried to live, and succeeded, but paid for it with my soul. One day the time just came, and I knew it, just as if my soul suddenly woke up and told me.

When I left I didn't take much with me. All I wanted was my life back. I didn't know where I would go, or how, but there was one thing I was sure of: *I deserve to have a life too.*

I stepped off the precipice of that life into a terrifying free-fall into darkness, emptiness, and the unknown. My soul said clearly, *"This must be done."*

I opened my eyes, and jumped.

I floated helplessly for a year, like an astronaut outside the ship in empty space, attached to any firm reality only by a thin lifeline that might at any moment dissolve. My sense of self was a blank page. It took time to re-gather and reclaim my own mind, but I did, and *I began to feel again.*

I took charge of my life again.

I got a divorce and I took back my own name.

I bought myself a really nice pair of cowboy boots.

18. I Don't Know A Thing About Love

We turn to love like sunflowers.
– Anne Lamott, from Small Victories

I don't know a thing about love. Never did. Nobody does really. We imagine something that's magically sublime, and then when something even more wonderful than that happens, we call it love. We are beyond ourselves with joy, immersed in happiness that goes all the way to our bones, and we want that feeling to last forever.

Usually it doesn't, but once in a while, it does, and then all the rest of us sigh in awe of those two rare people in our world who actually did find that kind of love. The kind where both are loving and both are loved, and they cherish each other all the rest of their lives. Mother and Daddy had that, and I think my teenage girlfriend Mary Frances' mother and dad had that.

I do know about lovemaking. I learned later than some, but in my life's adventures, I would both give and receive physical love very sincerely, even some times when it didn't last and I knew it wouldn't.

I married too young. I thought I loved him, I supported him, I was the good wife. I gave him my life, he took it for granted and wasted most of it. Looking back, it seems like he tossed out the best parts of me like the coffee grounds. That was my mistake, I admit. And those were the loneliest four years of my life.

After that, I felt so broken, I thought I would never find a way to love and *be* loved at the same time. But after another five years of slow healing, I did. Together we had a beautiful love, body, mind, and spirit, that lasted for seven years.

And then it shattered like one of those pretty crystal orbs from the Christmas tree, falling onto a hard stone floor in a quiet explosion everyone else hardly noticed, and breaking into bits so finely fragmented that they could never be put back together again, like a poof of dust almost. Simply gone. I had wanted it to last forever but it didn't. It couldn't.

The only thing I know for sure about love is, love is still the best feeling in the whole wide world. I have never felt so joyous, ever in my life as I did then, when I was loved. And giving never feels as good as it does when you're giving from love. When I lost the man who loved me like that, the pain of it was immense, oceanic. The air I breathed, hurt. It took much longer this time to heal, and it left new scars. But if I had it all to do over again, I would still do it.

We learn or don't learn how to love from our parents. That can be their greatest gift to us, but sometimes they don't have that themselves, and they can't give us what they don't have, though they would if they could. That makes it harder for some of us, a lot of us. We have to figure it out for ourselves. We make mistakes.

It's a good thing to love, and it's a good thing to be loved, and because of who we are, human beings, we will always seek for love the way flowers lean toward the sunlight and follow it across the sky. It's the nature of things.

If you can get some love, you should. If you can give some love, you should, even if those two things don't come at the same time. If you can have both at the same time, you are the two most blessed beings on the whole planet. Don't expect it to last forever, don't require it to, but always believe it might. Then cherish every day, every little moment of it.

My Mother and Dad are gone now, out there in the cosmos somewhere, but they're together, and still loving each other, truly forever. It is not impossible.

19. Who We Are

I've read that each of us, in our individual lives, are like a single cell of the cosmos, a cell in the body of God, only we don't know it.

My physiology book says: Cells have an outer layer that is a "permeable membrane," a kind of barrier, but through which some things, like fluid, nourishment and even bacterial invaders, can pass in and out. Every kind of cell is a part of, but never apart from, the body and all of its other cells, in a symbiotic relationship. That means they all need and benefit each other. In a similar way, I've also learned, and I believe this, that each of us is a unique but integrated consciousness, a cell in the Mind-Body of a conscious universe.

I think about us, each a component of a greater whole, and yet how different we are, like the cells of the human body, each of which has its own specific function and purpose for being, and relationship with all the other cells. I have often said, "We all come here to this life both to teach and to learn, knowingly or unaware, and to discover who and what we are." To do this, we need each other. Every one of us has a job here that matters to the whole of it all, in ways we may never see.

For my part, I have often blundered and stumbled in life, but mostly moved innocently and trustingly along. There have been some dark and painful times, but when I came through them to the other side, I always found that I was stronger and wiser because of them. There have been times I danced and laughed and loved, beautiful and young. Other times I may have been too much alone, and yet I scattered my love anyway like wildflowers along the road. As a child, I rejoiced running through the rain. As an adult, the spirit of me still does.

One of my sisters has lived her whole life not consciously aware. She's a good person, kind and content. She still lives in the same tiny Texas town, for some forty years now, and is very active in church and community. She is like a flower in a small protected garden, never exposed to too much life, and she is happy. She's a daisy who believes she is a rose, and as such she is proud and satisfied. She believes she has the best in life, and so, she does.

Believing is the master key. Both a blessing and a curse, it's a law of the universe and it's the one capacity that most shapes our physical life and experiences. Whether the particular belief itself is false or true, it becomes our truth, and our perceived reality. Then our lives play out from those core-beliefs, most of which were learned in the first five years of life. Because they operate below our conscious awareness, we can't change them unless we realize them and one day ask ourselves, Is this who I really am? And then seek to know.

My brother never knew who he was. As a child, he was the favorite, the first-born, lavished with love and attention. He learned that he was special and entitled. He demanded what he wanted, and he got it, and this became the mind-set he carried all his life. It didn't always work as well when he grew up and he was no longer the prettiest baby on the block. But he still thought he was. The world didn't always treat him as special as he felt he deserved, and so he spent most of his life bitterly resentful.

He was good-looking and smart, a charming manipulator, supported and sustained by women – his mother, his sisters, all his wives, and his affairs. But I don't think he was ever satisfied or truly happy. Might he have turned out differently if he had not been "spoiled" as the old folks said? I wonder though, if maybe it goes deeper than that, if maybe our life-roles somehow are decided by our souls before birth.

My personality has been so different from my brother's. I can't claim credit for who I am, or call myself "a better person," but I am sincerely grateful that my soul chose this life and not one like his. As a child I always had to accept less, but I'm wiser now. I see that really, I was the lucky one.

It didn't look so great for me at first. In my family I was the second-born, second-best. My brother was the pretty one, the dominant one, a relentless bully for whom I was "his personal punching-bag," as Granny said. She protected me from him and every other hurtful thing in my small new life. Mama didn't have time for me, she was too busy with my demanding brother, but I was happy enough to hang out with Granny. I didn't complain or expect anything more. I knew I was not special like my brother.

Life was not kind or generous to my birthmother Ann, She surely deserved better than she got. I never really knew her and she never knew me. It seems like her purpose in my life was to provide me with two profound things: a physical portal into this world, and my first great wound: unwantedness. There was no conscious decision on her part, no deep or personal intention, to do either of those things.

My true mother, Helen, was my rescuing Angel. She did not give birth to me, but she gave me life. I believe she was always meant to be my mother, and I am so grateful for this immense life-gift of grace. She's gone now, and my heart aches with a sweet sad joy when I think of her. The million little things she taught me still show up in my life every day, and she is right here.

My Dad was a good man, beautiful in both body and soul. He was a private person, gentle, modest, a man of few words, and a closet poet. Nobody knew him well, except Mother. Her love brought him out of his inner solitude and into a new openness and expression of himself to all of us who loved him.

These are some of the people who came and went through my "permeable membrane" of existence here on the pretty little blue planet where we live, swimming in the Milky Way Galaxy, circling one of its smaller stars. What I learned from these people has been absorbed and assimilated into my own being now, some of it consciously, and some of it still below my conscious awareness. I believe that everyone in our life is our teacher, and we too are teachers in theirs.

Oh Life, what a magnificent mystery you are! With infinite numbers of stories intersecting, paralleling for a while, and then diverging off into inexplicably interconnected paths. Some of the stories are beautiful and some are tragically not, and only the Author of Life itself knows their full meaning.

20. Writing Green

This title comes from a paragraph in Tobias Wolff's memoir, *This Boy's Life*. What a book it was! He wrote:

> *"When we are green, still half-created, we believe that our dreams are rights, that the world is disposed to act in our best interests, and that failing and dying are for quitters. We live in the innocent and monstrous assurance that we alone, of all the people ever born, have a special arrangement whereby we will be allowed to stay green forever."*

In this book the author wrote about his young mistakes and misdeeds with insightful candor and plainspoken honesty. He showed us through his child's-eye-view the shrewd, resourceful, and enterprising ways he messed up as a kid. Reading it, we can see his innocence, and recognize the same kind of unaware authenticity we all had when we were so young. The wonder is that as an adult writer, he has not lost that.

This is how one becomes great I think, by making many mistakes as young as possible, while there is still a good chance for forgiveness and enough time for reprieve as we learn about life and humanity from those mistakes.

Wolff's memoir is a beautifully unique book. Recently I reread it the third time, and I slowed myself down and tried to look at how he achieved so much depth and simplicity at the same time. He tells the truth with the perspective of a young-boy's naiveté, yet with the acute accuracy, insight, and vivid descriptive images of a brilliant storyteller. The book's subtle philosophy is never stated outright until this paragraph in the last chapter. Reading it, I lit up with desire like a firestorm jumping a 4-lane highway; I wanted to write something wonderful too.

As wonderful as his book? Maybe not, but the gauntlet had been thrown. I must do something as wonderful as I can. After reading this, nothing less than my best work, my deepest simplest truth, my most earnest honesty is good enough to make the working-draft, and then I will work to make it better.

I think the essence of memoir and its one sacred quality is its truth. Reading something that we know is one human being telling the truth about what life is, and what it means to be human, that's the gold standard, that's what matters the most.

In this cyber-age, the past which is the great teacher that could save us from blind self-destruction, now is widely ignored. The present, which in reality is the only time we actually have, goes disregarded by most, in favor of techno-fantasies. Life goes by, with millions of us not even noticing.

I know this: Something real of human value is badly needed for the survival of humankind. Not just the body, but the mind and perhaps even the soul of us, is in deep trouble.

The tide must turn, and writers have a responsibility in this. We are, after all, the light-bringers, aren't we? The pendulum must swing, and even though it is terrifyingly slow, I can see it beginning to move. People *want the truth.*

Truth has become extremely rare, much more rare than diamonds and infinitely more valuable. Lies have become the commonest coin of trade. We who write, whether memoir or fiction, which has valid truths of its own, must tell whatever truth we have, as honestly as we can, because in all the history of humankind, it has never mattered so much.

21. How To Retire

Retirement, from day one, was not what I expected. The usual concept of retirement suggests a sudden deluge of feelings of loss and separation, disconnection from routine and friends. The parameters of your life do change; that's for sure. For a lot of people they narrow or close down. Mine didn't. Mine opened up suddenly and vastly like a Montana sky at sunrise.

I was surprised that I didn't miss my day-job, my career, as much as I thought I would. Instead I felt an across-the-board elation and a surge of energy. It was not so much the end of a thing, but a graduation, and it felt right, even though it meant leaving a way of life I had loved. I didn't miss, as badly as I expected, the thing I thought I would miss the most – my friends. The best of them are still with me in person or by e-mail and internet. Some others, I realize now, were mostly circumstantial friends. They were true ones, but they came with the job and went with the job.

What's missing from my life now is the immense pressure and stress of the job itself, and that is, as my granny Vaughn used to say, "a good miss." Letting go of the position that had defined and confined me for 20+ years felt like lifting the lid off a boiling pot, and the pressure beneath it evaporating into the limitless free air.

Waking-up into "retirement" was a surprise, and the most surprising part: I had expected a period of depression in the transition. It never happened. What happened instead was a strange flowing immersion in warm happiness. Strange because it had no definable cause or object, simply no reason not to be, and I kept catching myself with a silly smile on my face.

I had been set free from a set of constraints and rules, the chain of command of managers, the requirement to smile no matter what, and to do what was expected of me flawlessly. All of that vanished in a day. *I own myself again, lock, stock, and barrel. I own my own life.*

I won't have as much money, but the trade-off is a terrific deal, "100% off." The new life is completely mine. Suddenly I'm as free as I was in my twenties but wiser and better financed. Then I lived on nearly nothing. Today my modest income does have its limitations, but is the bedrock of just-enough.

The first thing I did was take two weeks to relax and do whatever I chose to do in a totally un-rushed and un-pressured way. I took day trips and hikes in state parks. I cut my hair. I gave away my racing bike and bought a new one less flashy and more appropriate for my age. I spent long leisurely lunches chatting with friends. I wrote in my journal. I cleared my desk, purged some files, and caught up on correspondence. I filed that pile of mystery-stuff in my bulging To-File folder, then started calmly working through the formerly dreaded To-Do folder. Some of the to-dos had been there for years and now were either already done or obsolete.

The days rolled by seamlessly, pleasurably, in blissful sunny weather that's normal for winter in Northern California. Now I wake up to simple pleasures every day. I don't have to change clothes or personalities to suit my career any more. I don't have to drive on any freeway unless I want to, and never in commute-hours. I no longer put myself into any environment that's toxic or dangerous to me physically. All of that is behind me now, completely and well done. In our careers as Emergency Room Caregivers, my colleagues and I made meaningful contributions to each other and to humankind.

For most of my life I've done more than one thing – my day job, and on the side some other things I loved that were not practical. That is, they didn't generate income, but they gave me a lot of simple joy and a place to express. Now I take up my new role of writer and teacher. There's the memoir, a book of essays, and a chapbook of poetry and short stories in the works. I have plenty to do.

How to retire? I have no idea. I'm making it up as I go along. I suggest that it's good to have something on the side that you can move to the middle when you let go of the railings of your day job. If you're fortunate enough to be fairly healthy and agile, a whole new world is going to open up before you. You may find, as I did, that the experience feels like you have spent most of your life within a brightly-lit tunnel, through the years staying to the route, opening door after door, advancing through to more doors, and then suddenly one day you open *this* door, and find yourself outside . . .

And shocked to discover that it's not fearful or empty at all. It's alive with wind and sun and brilliant colors. There are real people here and plenty of work to do. Unknown new adventures are opening to you, and beckoning.

Start anywhere. Start where you are and dream big. Nobody can tell you who to be anymore; nobody can criticize or fault you for not being just exactly what they expect. You own yourself. You are free. Your heart floats, weightless as a sparrow in crystal blue morning air, and the sky is not the limit.

22. Writing Your Memoir

"Everyone should do this," I tell people, but with the caveat that "You probably should not do it until you're at least 50 years old, because you might not be able to handle it."

It's no small deal. To tell your truth honestly and earnestly means time-travel. Not just remembering it, *you have to go there.* This requires becoming a disembodied observer who looks down objectively, like a documentary filmmaker, or maybe a holy voyeur. You will see things you never saw about your life, yourself, and the people along your path. Truths and revelations you could not have seen with younger eyes.

Warning: This will sometimes be very painful. It will also be healing. Old wounds you didn't realize you still had will open up again right before your eyes. They may bleed and leak other nasty stuff you never knew was in there. That's the bad news. The good news is, you will also see other things that you didn't notice before: the beauty of yourself and other "imperfect" souls in your story. I promise you, you'll be astonished, and possibly overcome with love and respect for that stumbling, blundering, courageous innocent seeker-traveler that *you really were all the time.*

Emotional wounds are like abscesses, they scar-over with guilt and denial, but still enclose the same infected unhealthy stuff. When opened again in a clean place with a good light, they have the opportunity to drain their poisons and finally heal. But the way to healing will hurt.

We all have old wounds from our earliest years on earth. This simply goes with the life-path. A big part of the adventure in life is the challenge of managing your wounds, and not letting them manage *you.* But first you have to become aware of them. As you do, you will notice right away that there is nobody else who is not wounded too.

A friend of mine said, "But if so much of this stuff is unconscious, and it's been in there all your life, you can't really do anything about it, can you? You just have to let it ride."

Well, you will, *if that's what you choose to believe.* My friend was looking for a balance sheet, a bookkeeper-God. That's a one-sided mindset that takes you in circles.

On the other hand, you could seek to know what's down there in the dark hiding places of your own heart and mind, because when you see it, you have the power to make different choices now, than the ones you made in the past. You will see that you really are wiser now, just by living and learning in your life. When you see some of the things you have hidden, to protect yourself from them, you can own them as yours. Then you will have the power and the authority to change them. (I'm not saying any of this will be easy.)

Writing a memoir is a good way of looking at such things. But remember that to be of value, a memoir must *not be about judging* anything, or about getting revenge or retribution. It's you, telling the truth about *you.* It's got to be only what you experienced, and how that felt for you. These are not just facts, but truths. Others who were there, in the same time and place, will have almost certainly seen it differently than you did, that's just the way it is. That is their perception, their truth, not yours. You are not responsible for what they think or feel about it. That's *their* story. There is no real comparison here at all.

Memoir is the great cathartic self-reveal, where we finally, privately, (for we can always edit) can stand emotionally and spiritually naked and know it's okay. We will discover that we were innocent most of the time, and maybe some of the others in our life were too.

Telling the truth forces us to *re-open time,* and to look at ourselves and others in our story with mercy and compassion. It puts whatever regret or guilt we have been carrying into a truer perspective. Then we can see what to let go of because we never meant any harm in the first place. And maybe, neither did they. Discovering this was a great relief for me. I found that when I could honestly forgive, I could finally let myself be forgiven. Then the story was complete and the book could begin.

23. The Writer's Calling

Everyone writes in one way or another. It's just natural, like singing in the shower or dancing in the den when nobody's around. Writers write because we must. We write whether we get published or not, whether we even want to get published or not. Writing, like singing, dancing, is natural human expression. All children do it, until they're told to choose something grown-up to do.

What we write may be light and uplifting, or it might be fraught with a reality too painful to confess aloud, but too damaging to keep inside. Whether it's entertaining or profound with meaning, each way caries its own gift. Sometimes there are hard parts, and you don't want to go there. Nevertheless you know you have to bring whatever light you have, whatever you have been given, to share. The sharing of it usually comes not from a choice, but from an inner need or *calling*, to tell it.

We can only write from who we are, even when we write fiction. If that's what we've been given, that's what we've got to give. There is always a human truth in fiction, even beneath the conscious awareness of the writer. Truth can be dangerous, and often unbeautiful. Your truth might not be everybody's cup of tea.

When you think about it, reading a book is a journey we take in consciousness. That's what it is, no matter what reason we opened the first page. There have been books I've started to read and then stopped. Intuition, that little voice from the inside, told me there might be glimpses of truths I wasn't ready for yet, or things that would hurt me by reopening old wounds, and so I chose not to go there, yet. If you write a book, and set it loose in the wild world, be aware that your personal world around you may not be ready or eager to hear this part of you.

The literary memoir I'm writing has some dark passages. A

few old friends started to read it and then stopped when they got to the hard parts. I want everybody to love my book, but I know that not everybody will. Books that tell the truth always make people uncomfortable. Like life, reading a book all the way through takes commitment, even courage, to push on through, all the way to the end. The Whole Truth. It takes even more courage for the writer, because we have to go through it over and over, weeding out the less-important bits, and judging every line:

"Is this clear? Is this honest? Is this still true on a wider perspective than just my own life? Is this as good as it can be? Is it good enough?"

A book can claim you. This memoir has done that. I can clearly see that all the events of my life, even the worst of them, have had a purpose, and whate I've learned from them, I have a responsibility to share. The time has come to do the work, and I have said yes.

This has turned out to be much harder than I thought it would be, even though I knew it would be hard. When I write, my brow is furrowed, my back muscles knot painfully, my neck is tense. No muse whispers inspiration in my ear, no choir of angels sing sweetly from a convenient cloud. *And yet, there are moments...*

There have been unexpected gifts, bursts of epiphany or fierce clarity that appear all at once, unexpectedly, like a silent soft explosion. There are times when I truly *see*.

Sometimes in the morning I start writing and then all of a sudden I notice that the sun is going down. Those are the times Life is using me. I know that I'm just the pen and ink. Whatever is true comes *through* me, not *from* me. My job is to write it down.

24. The Path: Life After Life

My nearly-lifelong best friend developed Alzheimer's much too young. When she began to leave us behind. It was painful for all of us who loved her. We were many, and we loved her so much. Lynn was the most joyful person I ever knew, intrepid explorer and adventurer of the outdoors, always the first one up the next new trail.

Physically she lingered here for several more years, but she was soon gone from us in almost every other way. She didn't recognize us. She didn't remember us. She was confused, and she was afraid. Lynn had never been afraid in all her life before. Our hearts were crushed.

When the time came, she passed away gently in sleep. In some sort of way I can't explain, we accepted it, almost as a sweet relief. We cried for ourselves, but we didn't cry for Lynn. She was free again.

She had outrun us again. Always out ahead of us, the fearless trailblazer. She still is, just on a trail we can't follow as closely now, but someday will. She's free now to discover new trails, explore new adventures as she has always loved to do.

She was too young, so full of life, we said, and my heart cried out, *Why do things like this happen?* But I knew that God/ Spirit/ Universal Consciousness doesn't like Why-Questions, there will always be things we can't understand. But I'm beginning to feel some sense of it all, and stop struggling to figure everything out.

I've come to believe there are some things we simply are not given to know. God knows, and watches out for us, and I see the proof of this everywhere in my own life. But God, whatever that is, also allows us to wander if we choose, to explore, and even to blunder off the path, lets us stumble as we are learning how to run, but never lets us stray too far.

If we lose our way, or if we hunger for a greater challenge than this life holds for us, God can always call us home. Then in the morning, we begin again.

25. Carousel and Candle

I think we surely must be God's most extravagant experiment, because He made sure to provide us with every unimaginable experience with which to discover ourselves while we're here. This Life is a glorious circus parade, passing through endless landscapes and cities, a carnival of lights and colors, wonderful rides and unlimited games to enjoy.

Most of all, Life is a marvelous ride, like the ones I loved as a child on the beautiful life-sized hand-carved and painted horses of the old carousel at the Texas state fair. I thrilled at the surging flight of my noble steed, rising in slow-motion leaps and bounds, sailing me through the air, up and down and gracefully forward in rhythm with the strange haunting calliope music that only carousels have.

I was the brave and joyful master of it all. *I could really fly.* It felt wonderful, completely magical. And when the music stopped and the wheel of charging horses slowed down, for another ten cents I could stay on and ride again, another ride, another tune, another flight of happiness.

Now that I'm grown, I know too much to be quite as happy as that, or as carefree as that, and I know my ride will not go on forever, but I have not forgotten how it felt to be magic.

The time will come for each of us when we will step down from the merry-go-round, and it will go on without us. With all the bright colors and calliope music, the beautiful horses will surge onward, up and down, round and round, and will not miss a beat. In the midst of all of this marvelous life, who will notice that we are gone?

If someone blows out a candle at noonday, who can see that it is gone? Who will know, and miss its light? Only the one who is holding it, and the one who blows it out. Only the people who loved us, and God.

26. Telling The Truth

Telling the truth means telling the plain truth, life as it is, or was, without rounding off some edges to make it look better, or sharpening them to look worse. In life as it is, some of it will be warm and sweet, some will be jagged as shattered glass.

Broken families scatter their children's lives across a broad landscape of uncertainty, confusion, and often despair. Our first five years are the time we are getting our first learnings about who we are and where we fit into the world, and it's harder to know who we are if we have known only one of our parents, or perhaps neither. We can only guess.

We assume that however the big people around us are, parents or strangers, that's the way people are supposed to be, and how *we* are supposed to be. But we do not fail to know, even as children, *that's not who we are.*

Life is complex; we try to understand. We accept from the world outside us things that are not true, and we come to believe them. Then what we believe creates who we are and what we do in the world. Somehow we know that the truth of is deeper, but we're scared to go there to find out. Nobody told us we should.

At some point we begin to need to know who we really are, our genuine authentic self, apart from what the world expects or demands for us to be. So we begin to seek the truth beneath the surface of circumstance. *What really matters? Do I matter?*

The deeper we venture into the ocean of our own soul, seeking to understand who we are, the more currents and undercurrents we will feel and be affected by. Our history and the history of our family, our wounds, and our scars. This is why we all fear to enter our own depths. And yet, that's where the truth is, and that's where the healing is.

"Our wound is the place where the light enters us." — *Rumi*

27. The Way

What life is about is as many things as there are lives, but there are some basic essentials of foundation, framing, and scaffolding that naturally occur in the universe to shape the structure of it and hold it all together.

We're standing here while our pretty little planet goes spinning around, circling our star, one of the billions of stars in this and other galaxies, and all of this is operating with exquisite precision, a cosmic clockworks more vast and complex than the human mind will know for a few billion more years, if we last that long as a species. Homo sapiens is a very young species. Cockroaches for example, are more evolved, with millions more generations of adaptation than we have. But we are special because we can think bigger thoughts than they can.

Essential to human evolution is the process of lessons and learnings, endeavors and outcomes, emotional wounds and scars. Wounds can heal, but scars are forever a reminder of the lessons we learned or failed to learn, as my Dad used to say "the hard way." Everything that happens has meaning and purpose, often unknown to us, invisible at close range, and only seen when looking back from a distance. Then the patterns can be seen apart from the confusing colors, shapes, and lines of circumstance, cause, and blame.

The soul always has a plan that the mind can't see. Those who follow the soul's illogical calling arrive safe and sacred at the goal that this life intended. Those who stick too close to what the world expects, may not get there, unless we are rescued by grace from our mistakes and given another start, or several. It seems to come down to this:

There is a path. Find it, and walk forth through light or darkness, sun or rain. Teach and learn from each other, for all have a gift to give, and this is what you came here for.

28. All I Truly Am

"Whenever we deny the negative aspects of ourselves, we try to overcome them by becoming their opposite. We create entire personas to prove to ourselves that we are not that."
–The Dark Side Of The Light Seekers, Deborah Ford

I must confess to this. I've built several personas and several careers in my life so far. For one of them, I became a firefighter after having been victimized, terrorized, bullied and abused by my older brother who taught me that I was weak and helpless. It wasn't true, but the circumstances seemed to prove it. I also was repeatedly told by my family that everything I loved, "You can't have that/ do that/ be that, because you're a girl." Maybe I needed to prove I could. Or maybe I was looking for brothers to make up for the one I didn't have. As a firefighter, I got myself some, about 40 of them. Some of them liked me and some didn't, but I had a badge and a chance. I worked hard and smart, and I got promoted to lieutenant.

It felt great to express my strength and intelligence and other things that always were disallowed to me before. It felt good to take charge and be a leader, no longer a victim always having to defer to everyone else. I was still obedient, but to the chain of command, our purpose, and our Fire Department. I was part of a team, doing things that mattered.

I loved the strenuous physical work, feeling the surge of my own strength and ability. I found out *I don't have to be weak,* that was a lie too. I did the work to make myself strong, and I got strong. I discovered that I was stronger than many who were much bigger than I was. They were bigger in size, but nobody was bigger than me in courage and determination. I was smart, and I had agility and endurance.

I learned how to fight. Fires, fears, stereotypes. prejudices, and adversaries. It felt good to take serious risks and face big challenges, to meet the other side of myself that I had always been told I could not and should not be. I served for eight and a half years as a line firefighter. It was a wonderful adventure, and it proved that the meanest lie of all was not true. The truth is, and always was, *girls can.*

In my next career I would become almost the opposite, a hospital Emergency Room ER Tech, always smiling, always serving. I was learning to surrender in the right way, for the right reasons. I learned to care and protect, to help and to heal, and did so for 20 years. Now that career has been completed, and the task of this time in my life is to continue to discover and to become as much as I can of what I really am. This is true of all of us, and so, for as long as we are alive in this place, we are still *becoming.* For all of us there is more to learn, more to do that matters, and more to be. I can see clearly now, that *I am all of those things I learned.* Both warrior and healer. Fighter and caregiver. I know how to be both powerful and compassionate.

I'm now in my third career. When I made the commitment to write my the memooir, something happened. A small cog somewhere in the immense clockworks of the universe clicked-over one tiny notch, and my life began to turn, and to make more sense. All the parts of it, so different, began to fall into place. I saw that all of it had meaning and value for me, even the parts I had judged as weaknesses, mistakes, or failures.

"When you don't own an aspect of yourself, it runs your life," The author Deborah Ford said. I know that was a big part of what Fire Service was for me: owning and facing the hated role of weak helpless victim, challenging it, *and changing it.*

Best of all, on top of my pure and deep love of Fire Service itself and all the other good things it gave me, there was the delicious pleasure of doing what everybody said I couldn't do, and said I couldn't be. But look – I did. I am.

29. Bridges / Changes

In this life there are bridges of time and destiny that connect the present to the future, the known to the unknown, and the seen to the unseen. For each of us, decisions must be made, and some of them will be hard.

When you stand on a bridge of steel and concrete, there are three choices. You can choose to stride forward, you can turn back, or you can jump off. But in the living of a lifetime, the choices are more subtle and less clear. We live encapsulated in linear time, so we can't go back, and we are always crossing in the dark.

When life changes, you will have to let it change, even if you don't want it to, for it will change no matter what.

Your soul's success depends both on what you do and how you hold yourself as you do it. You can resist the change, or you can choose to go with the tide of it, and see where it takes you. This will sometimes be frightening, and inevitably it will bring more decisions and choices: to stay or to go, to resist or to surrender, to stand your ground or to escape. We will all make choices like these, over and over, along our life-journey.

In this life *we are always leaving something.* That's a given. There is a difference between running away and moving on, and it's not about winning or losing. Places, things, and times in life will all come to their resolution and end, and when they are done, they must be released. Some of them will be ready to be freed, and yet we will hang onto them. We fear or dread to leave what is over, because letting go would feel like a loss, and moving on might be dangerous and insecure. But the dilemma then is that we are stuck and we can't cross over into the next new life-experience.

There's another option, one that empowers us to keep going

forward even through our life's greatest challenges, obstacles, perceived failures and endings. It has been called many names. I love this one, Marianne Williamson called it "transcendence," and she said it this way:

"*Rise above the battlefield, strong and magnificent.*

In some difficult, even agonizing problems, challenges and endings of my life, I did not feel anything like "strong and magnificent." I felt small and ashamed, abandoned and afraid, hurt and angry at myself, or someone else, or both. There were too many times when I felt helpless and victimized and wronged, and circumstantially, that was true.

But the circumstances of our lives are just the chutes and ladders, hurdles and footraces of it. *We are not that.* I am not, and you are not. Circumstance is really only the backdrop of our lives, the landscape that's constantly changing. The real energy and movement of life is deeper, stronger, quieter, and more permanently anchored in our authentic Self. One thing is very clear: *We are not our circumstances. We can move above them, and eventually we will always move past them.*

Life is bigger. We are bigger, stronger, and more free than we have the ability to know now, with only the limitations of this human mind. The times when I have somehow had the courage to trust in this, to trust life, to trust God and step forward even when I was afraid, there was always someplace to go. Even if I could not see it yet, there was something more. With every leaving, there was an arriving. There was a new learning that would eventually bless me. However daunting the crossing was, I found out I could make it.

Whatever seems to be stopping you now, nothing can stop your soul from overcoming it. Whatever comes up to challenge us, even in the hardest times, and especially then, we are growing.

30. Grace, The Gift Unasked For

On a pale cold not-quite-spring day in Minneapolis, I wandered downtown alone with no place to go and feeling as bleak as the empty grey sky. Up ahead on the sidewalk coming from the opposite direction towards me, came a young couple, obviously in love, striding along with their arms around each other's waist. It was a time when my own life was shattered. At twenty-six I was just-divorced, lost, confused, a thousand miles from home and family ties, and the loneliest I had ever been in my life. The hopes I'd had for love and for life, now were nothing but ashes.

The two young people came swinging along down the sidewalk toward me, and suddenly for no reason, at the same moment they both looked up at me and smiled.

I felt it – like a wave of warmth. Amazed. Such a small gift, but in that one moment, it blew open my heart like a gust of summer, and completely transcended the sorrow.

I felt my heart lift up, like a sparrow startled into flight, and in that instant, I knew that life had not forsaken me entirely. There would be another chance for me, and although *I can't say how I knew this,* I knew it to the marrow of my bones.

The book A Course in Miracles says, "There are no accidents and no coincidences." I had been given a glimmer of grace, by two people who would never know me or ever see me again. They had no way of knowing that they had lifted me out of my desolate hopelessness with their simple openhearted act, spontaneously sharing with me, just for that moment, the joyful love they felt for each other.

Tears stung my face as I walked to the bus stop. I could feel the icy air begin to freeze the tears, and I laughed. I walked on, and the cold was starting to make my face a little stiff, just enough that I could feel it smiling.

31. Remembering Winter

Minnesota winters, people hide indoors and the life outside goes underground. Plants drop back to earth, where the silent pulse of them withdraws to deep roots beneath sheltering snow. In the wild places, bears retreat to their woodland dens to sleep, and squirrels to their nests.

I sit and read good books by my fire, while outside the snow drifts are heaped up above the porch steps. The killing cold is 17° below zero, the trees are thrashing and breaking their brittle arms in storm winds, while the remorseless weather howls and moans like an injured beast that cannot die.

These are times, says the I Ching, when "waiting is the course that brings success." I am not just waiting though, I am thinking. Wondering. Planning. I am trusting that the summer will come again, and when it does, I will be ready.

32. Roberto

In the Oncology unit, there were many patients that we could not save, then we had to let them slip away from our memory because we couldn't carry around all those souls and all those stories inside of us. As caregivers and professionals, we all knew this, and yet there were some who claimed a spot in our hearts and minds that couldn't be denied.

This was my first hospital job, I worked two years as a Patient Care Assistant on the nursing staff in the cancer ward. It was hard, but it was a deep education, and the best possible preparation for the physical and emotional challenges that would be routine in the next phase of my career, ER. In oncology I met some of the noblest expressions of humanity, people who lived and died with great courage, dignity and honesty.

Roberto was one of the eight or ten patients a day I was assigned to care for. Right from the start, he stood out. Though he was diagnosed with stage-4 terminal cancer, he seemed more well than he was. Always quietly kind and cheerful, his presence was one of peacefulness and serenity. He was a strong-looking Jamaican man in his 50s, with an athletic build and a very gentle nature. Sometimes he shared his thoughts with me as I made his bed and brought a fresh hospital gown and towels for his bath. He was very health-conscious, and he seemed to have a fatherly concern for all the nurses and aides. He told me once, "When you shower, take a fresh lemon cut in half. After you bathe and your skin is still wet, rub the lemon over all of your body, then a light rinse. It will refresh your body and your spirit as it returns the balance of acid to your skin."

I never thought that I was anything special to him, no more than any other nurse or housekeeper or aide; he was always friendly and kind to everyone.

I wasn't there when he passed, one evening on the night shift. The next morning when I came to work, the night nurses told me that when he was dying, he had asked for me. I was surprised, and deeply moved. That was the first time I realized, profoundly, that we never really know who we might be to someone, or how we might matter to them.

Roberto's soul had left a soft mark on me. I began to feel a little bit differently about a lot of things. I dared to risk caring a little more deeply about my patients, especially the angriest, most difficult ones. Many of the patients were terminal, and each time another one was lost, when I got home after work I allowed myself a space of time to cry a little and say a prayer of farewell for them. In oncology I learned a lot of lessons about life, and one of the most important ones was that small things matter, and even the simplest gestures of love are never wasted.

Roberto had been a natural philosopher and mystic. Some of the things he said struck me so deeply that I remembered them, and when there was a moment in my rushed and never-done-soon-enough work, I wrote them down to save. One of those times he had said to me:

> "Where we are now, we're only here for a little while. Each life has a time of beginning and a time of end, and our soul has chosen both. This sojourn here is not all we have forever, there is much more beyond what we can see. But eternity is too wide and too high for us to bear, as we are now. It's one of the rules of the game that we decided to play before we came, and then we forgot we were playing, and forgot it was only a game. We all forgot that we are divine and forgot what we knew before we came here—that there are an infinite number of games to play and ways to dance and songs the spirit sings."

33. Saying Yes To The Calling

Who knows what sets it off? It can be any unexpected thing. Maybe something happens in your life, like an accident, an illness, or an unexpected change. It could be something wonderful or something tragic, or it could be what seems like a small thing, something you hardly notice at all, nothing you can name, but suddenly one day your eyes open in a different way. One day you realize, *I am not nothing, I matter.* And that in fact, you are something profound.

This experience of "waking up" will be both marvelous and terrifying, because you will realize that it's time for you to stand up and hold up your little candle and share your light, whatever light you have.

We all stumble at the brink of this, hesitant and uncertain. The real fear is not the standing up, for we have done that before. The real fear is that the candle we've been given may not be as little as we thought.

34. The North Shore

The first time I came to the North Shore of the Mendocino Coast was when I had to leave the man I had loved for seven years and had intended to spend the rest of my life with. I felt desolate and lost, as if the ground had dropped out from under me. I needed to feel the solid living earth beneath my feet again.

The second time was when I had failed my first firefighter physical agility test, and I was drowning in shame. The third, when cancer obliterated my perfect plans for a future, redirected my path, and ultimately opened up the gift of a new life. The fourth was when 9/11 happened, and all of us were plunged into a bottomless pool of grief, fear, horror, and shock. And there have been a few more sojourns since.

Each of the times was different, but the purpose was the same. I came seeking a place of shelter and a time to heal. The outcomes would prove to be the same too: redemption and a silent reassurance. Each time the gift I needed was given to me: a new beginning.

Every time I go back to Mendocino County's rugged Pacific coast, the headlands and the redwood forests, it is a sacred journey. The patience and dignity of the ancient trees quietly seeps into my soul and comforts me. The rocky headlands, the sweet salt air, and the white-frothed breakers endlessly crashing, all of this fills me with exhilaration. I can feel the strength and power of the earth itself, it begins beneath my feet and rushes up through my body and into my soul.

At the edge of the Pacific Ocean, I stand in awe. I can see all the way to where the blue of sea blends flawlessly into the blue of sky. I marvel at how the edge of the shoreline yields and changes in the ocean's embrace. They are lovers, eternally joined. Even as the shoreline changes, the sea holds it gently and never lets it go.

All along the headlands I have found unspeakably beautiful places. One year, a narrow sandstone bar, a thin bridge of sandy rock, terrifyingly high above the crashing surf below. It was miraculously sprouted with unexpected bunches of wildflowers, defiant in the fierce winds, and living on only the moisture of evaporating ocean spray far below. Very carefully I made my way out onto it. There were places where it was less than two feet wide, and daringly I shot some breathtaking photographs.

When I came back to Mendocino a few years later, I looked for it again, but it was gone. I couldn't even be sure where it had been before, and nothing even resembled it. The sea had reclaimed it. Like so many things in this life, it looked like rock, but it was really only glory, being manifest for a while.

I know that this life we have is only a part of the infinite Ocean of Being. Sometimes it embraces us with tenderness, or challenges us with force and unexpected pain. We are ever changing and being changed through our eternal love-affair with Life. I believe this is how it's meant to be.

My advice to you as my fellow traveler here:

Pack light. See deeply. Miss nothing. Take pictures with your camera but also with your eyes, and save them forever in your heart and mind. Don't let anything beautiful slip by you without being seen and celebrated, for this moment is a gift. It is sacred and will never come again.

35. Believe Anyway

Even though it's true that every life will have some stumbling places, some dark passages and challenges to grow through, one of the most powerfully profound factors of truth is that *Life responds to our held-beliefs.* That's the catch-22 that our parents didn't teach us, because they didn't know.

For much of my adult life, I never asked for what I really wanted because I thought I didn't deserve it. Even if I prayed for it, I did so as a meek unworthy supplicant, not as a fully entitled child of the Most High, my Father God. Now I know why our prayers for other people so often are more successful than prayers for ourselves – it's because we dare to ask earnestly for their sake, in trust and faith, because we *believe* that they deserve it.

The teacher Jesus said, "Whatsoever you ask, believe you have received it, and it shall be yours," and He always said what he meant, and meant what he said. It *sounds* easy, but the catch is, you've got to somehow *dare to believe that you deserve it,* even if you don't. He tells us to believe that "even before you ask" the gift is already given, prepared for you, ready to go, with your name on it. You just have to believe it, to receive it. In this physical world, that seems absurdly unrealistic. And then Deepak Chopra says you must hold your desire in your heart with all your strength, *and then release it.* Toss it casually like a lateral-pass to Life/God/the Universe, then just relax and trust "it's on the way, done deal, no problem."

But wait a minute. If "The Force is always with us," then why don't we always get what we want? Because God/Life/ Universe/Great Consciousness, whatever name we use for the Life Force, always works to bring about what we are actually believing, and is not fooled by what we're just saying. Words have power, that's a fact. but nothing in the universe has as much power as faith. Believing right, or believing wrong, has equal power.

This process is real and eternally active. It's a life-law that anyone can use, and like the law of gravity, it works the same for everybody, and it works whether you notice it or or not.

You're free to choose the life you really want. Therefore by all means, do whatever you have to do *in order to believe in it, as rightly yours.* Begin to live as if it were so, even though it's not (yet). The saying, "Fake it till you make it" carries a grain of truth. The simple practice of "feeling-as-if" sends a positive message to the universe and moves you a little closer toward your wished-for self.

Whatever you habitually entertain in thought, worry, or expectation, life will habitually deliver to you. So be careful of what you are believing unaware, in the dark corners of your mind, for it is not harmless. Lies, when you believe them, are as powerful as the truth, because you are holding them as your truth.

Faith works. What we believe, we will receive. We often fail to have faith in the best things of life because there's always so much ugly "physical evidence" to the contrary on the 10 o'clock news. These are real people's lives, yes, but if you find yourself more blessed than that, don't feel guilty, *feel grateful.* You can't change all the troubles in the world, but you can make your choices different from the individuals on the news. When you choose health and happiness for yourself, you enable yourself to be more help to everyone else, and a more positive force in the world wherever you are, in whatever you do.

Search out, call forth, and shore up that hidden strength that's in you. Have the courage to believe in your own life and in your self, no matter what the odds are, no matter what other people's lives are, and no matter what other people say.

You've got to *be willing to believe* that God thinks you're good enough, even if you're pretty sure you're not. You've got to make up your mind, and then, as stubbornly determined as a four-year-old, *Believe Anyway.*

36. Macho / Macha

Does it seem like the males of our species accept the idea of killing or dying for honor more than the females of the species do? In many cultures, the glorious death is admired by heroic men, but women are not charged with this responsibility. I think we naturally tend to *live for, rather than die for,* what we believe in. I think maybe living for what you believe might be harder than dying for it. I mean, you only have to die once, but to live for what you believe means you have to gather your courage and confront the painful, the uncertain, and the unbearable, *every day, year after year,* without medals, flags, or banners of glory. Some men do that. Nelson Mandela, a man, was surely one of the most courageous people who lived for what they believed in. But the rules are still unclear.

Born a girl, I was taught to see myself as inferior, to respect all men more than women because of their presumed superiority in intelligence, bravery, and character. As I grew up, real life didn't always match up with that, yet I got passed over or denied what I wanted, even if I was good at it, because I was a girl. Especially the *brave* things, like cowboy, pilot, and firefighter. Mama said, "Those things are for boys."
I said, *"Why can't a girl be brave?"* I got no answer.

For me, the traditional kind of macho bravery seemed like a coat of bright paint, declaring itself with banners and badges, uniforms, boots and helmets, and who wouldn't want that? I did too.

But when I grew up, I learned that courage is different from bravery. Quieter, often unspoken and unrecognized. There have been times in history when women have matched men in courage, and if anyone deserves the Medal Of Honor for service and valor above and beyond the call of duty, mothers, daughters, sisters and grandmothers surely do.

In recent years, the truth has outed itself: *men are only people*. Not gods, not heroes, not magically superior beings as we were taught. It's no secret anymore. Maybe we have all done men a terrible injustice to demand so much more from them. Yet boys and girls are still taught this unachievable lie that has damaged all of us. Boys should always be the boss. We believed it because we were just kids, and the big people told us we should. *But honestly, just between me and you, didn't you always know it wasn't fair? And it wasn't even true?*

37. Forgiving

Forgiving seems like hard work. It seems so impossible, we don't want to go there. I didn't forgive my 2-year-old brother for trying to kill me when I was four days old and then continuing to terrorize me for the next 13 years of my life, until I was fifty-something. When we were both very young, he taught me to see my life through eyes of fear and weakness, and see myself as the rightful victim of his power. There were a lot of things I had to learn all over again as an adult. That could only happen after painfully unlearning the values I was taught as a child. It was hard work, work that hurt. And yet, this is the hallmark of a survivor: the ability to start over new and let go of what's past, especially everything that starts with "You can't ..."

The thing I most wanted to end, but couldn't get free of for decades into my life, was that role of victim. I knew from the start, *This is just wrong. I don't deserve this.* But my brother was allowed to abuse me and I was taught that this was okay because "Boys will be boys." I could escape him by running away, but that still rankled me. Even after I was old enough and left home, I carried a lingering fear and dread of him and people like him, who took advantage of me in life because, like wild dogs, they could smell the fear in me.

It would be many years before I realized that holding onto my resentment, my fear and my anger, was not hurting my brother a bit. It never had, it was only hurting me. That was the genius of his game: planting fear and resentment deep into his victims minds, to fester there forever.

Even after he was no longer in my life, the old scars would still sting whenever they were disturbed by some new small injustice, until finally something in me woke up. Maybe it was something I read in a book, but one day it just dawned on me.

Even when he is not hurting me, my own fear and rage are

still churning around inside me. I hate this. I don't want to live like this. I don't want to feel like this anymore.

I was about to discover something I never would have guessed: that applying the practice of forgiving can dissolve the oldest steel and rust of internal locks, and then when they crumble and fall away, *you have set your own self free.* So I set out to learn what this forgiveness thing was. It turned out that it wasn't what I thought.

Forgiving is not a thing you do because Jesus did it, (although, besides being a wise and loving teacher, he was also a sly and brilliant man) and it doesn't let the perpetrator off the hook. (Important note.) No, it's the way you get yourself off the hook, out of the trap. You can make the decision to walk away from the old self-hurting thoughts, fears, resentments, anger, shame, and other psychological bricks-in-the-backpack that someone else has planted there. You step out of "their" hold on you, the minute you realize that it was really only you, holding you.

"OKAY!" you will say. "DONE ! I forgive you right now, and I'm done with this! I'm canceling whatever it was, null and void. I choose to walk away from this, now and forever."

It turned out to be not that easy, but also not as hard as I expected. This time I saw the truth and I believed it. I didn't have to let the wrongdoing be okay, I just had to get up and walk away, and not take it with me. And I did. And then I said, right out loud:

I hereby know and declare: (in clear unequivocal terms):

I deserve to be free! I deserve to be happy! Nobody can MAKE me feel anything I don't want to feel! I own my mind. I can choose what I want to have in it.

I'm letting go of you and any hurts about you, right Now. Even if I wanted you before, I know now that I don't need you. I'm strong enough to stand up and let go, and walk away free.

Then as soon as you decide to end it, *it ends. Forever.* Healing will take some time, but in the meantime, give up the misery and refuse the pain. You don't deserve it and you don't need it.

38. The Little Gifts

Children speak their innocent wisdom like the wrens and finches in my lemon tree, utterly unaware that they are wise. Most of us, the grown-ups, don't notice the wisdom because, for one reason or another, we don't listen.

Got a minute? Stop and listen – to the voices and sounds of the children and grandchildren down the block playing, laughing, shouting, happily chasing each other, shrieking in delight or horror at finding an earthworm, quarreling over small things with large passion. Take a second to shamelessly eavesdrop on the squabbles of sparrows and bluejays. The bluejays may be bigger and more aggressive, it doesn't matter. The sparrows always win, because of their greater courage and numbers.

I laugh at the squirrels in the back yard chasing each other, scampering from the oak tree, across the fence on tiptoe like circus tightrope walkers, to the lemon tree, to the garage roof, to the apple tree next door. I envy them, they are so joyful. They run and play like children all their lives, totally innocent, and I realize that they are a nice little gift to me.

When I look, I can see all sorts of little gifts, already given to me. Given to all of us, but so many of them are never received because we hurry off to our work and our responsibilities without noticing. Maybe they are given to us exactly for that reason, because of all that work and responsibility – to lift and lighten the weight of it with moments of fun.

Don't walk away without noticing the smallest wonders. Enjoy everything. Grilling in the backyard, the neighborhood softball games, the wonderful awful laughable crazymaking things kids do as they are learning about life.

Appreciate the sweet earnest sincerity of your dumb but

lovable dog, and the quirky personality of your vain, smarty-pants cat. These, and all the other lovely small things a thoughtful God has scattered around in obvious places for us to discover, are gifts of great value. Don't throw away the little gifts, just because they're free.

39. The Leap

Another of my old team of work-friends has recently retired from the place I worked for 20 years and they for 30, a hospital Emergency Room. It's almost all new-blood now, new-grads fresh out of nursing school. Sometimes I have to wonder if the new ones go into the profession for the same reasons we did.

The old-timers, veteran caregivers like us, went into it mostly for the challenges and personal gratifications of serving humanity, pledged to be caregivers who actually cared. That seems to be going out of style, and when the mega-corporation took over our hospital, they used the word "customers" instead of "patients." In the last months before I turned in my security badge and keys, we were admonished to "Get in and out of the rooms as quickly as possible, so they don't ask you questions."

For the new professionals, within their working lifetimes things will change again, for better or worse. They will learn a lot from their patients, if they pay attention. They will learn much more than their teachers taught them in nursing school.

ER veterans are masters of compassionate learning. We've been forged on the front lines, in the trenches, dodging virtual bullets, sometimes real ones, and unexpected physical attacks and assaults of various kinds. One of the very first skills you learn as an Emergency Medical caregiver, whether in ER, Fire service, or ambulance, is to *jump back quick*, because all kinds of stuff can (and will) come flying at you without warning.

I loved my profession and the personally rewarding and fascinating work of the Emergency Room, but as in each of my earlier careers, the time came when I knew it was completed, and it was time to do something else with my life. And so after 20 years in ER, almost to the day, I silently gave myself permission to step out of the harness and set myself free, and then one day, I did.

Retirement from either Fire Service or hospital Emergency Services is a bit like an honorable discharge from the Army. You no longer wear a uniform: 1. dark blue shirt and pants and steel-toe fire-boots, or 2. baby-blue hospital scrubs and practical, silent, soft-soled white shoes. You don't have to 1. salute anybody and 2. you're no longer required to perpetually smile, maintain saintlike patience, and serve everyone. Now you can serve yourself. What an outrageous idea!

Now my new job is to tell stories that mean something, and life has given me an abundance of wonderful stories to tell. So here goes another career, another no-guarantee new beginning, and like all beginnings, this one also has some scary aspects. Courage was a primary requirement for both of the jobs I left behind, so I already know that courage doesn't mean you never have any fear, it just means you face it, and do what needs to be done, as well as you humanly can. All paramedics, firefighters, and ER nurses know this. You have prepared your skills, your strength, and your spirit. You know that if it can be done, you will do it.

So this is not really retirement. I call it a "vocation change." Women have many more choices than our grandmothers did. Many of us are beginning new careers, paid or volunteer, or starting new businesses. Some things we've been thinking about for years, now we have the opportunity to take a shot at. Professional careers are like a train on a track, you know where to go. But now you're cut loose, free in the world with no track, no map, just an open road. *Incredible!*

I gave myself a sabbatical year before making the decision to commit to the risks of another new career, to take myself seriously as a writer. The uncertainty is back. This is a leap of faith, and it's no cakewalk. I don't know exactly what I ought to be, or what I ought to look like. But life feels fresher, cleaner, and sort of wonderful. My confidence is returning, and as my energy grows, my spirit opens, and I notice that my new beginning is beginning to begin.

This has happened before in my life, so I know it's doable. The only question left to ask is: *Am I willing to go for it, all out, and seek "My Greatest Yet-To-Be"?*

It's not "Am I ready?" Nobody does great things by waiting until they're ready. It's "Am I willing? That's the LEAP. And yes, I am willing.

40. Compass Points

My road goes on. Some people I loved have passed on to whatever new adventures come after this earthly one that I'm still celebrating. I'm grateful for it, too. I've had some marvelous times, and I'm still having fun, so I'll stick around and see what happens next.

My sisters are happy and content in their tiny Texas towns. Both are widows now with grown children, lots of money, and nothing much to do. Over the holidays last year they took a Caribbean cruise, a thing I will probably never do in this lifetime. I don't mind.

My brother is single again after five marriages and five divorces. "I just haven't found the right woman" he says. All the endings of course were always the woman's fault. The years haven't changed him, he's still supported by women, but now they're nurses in a locked ward. He is well-fed, well-attended, and apparently happy. He still believes absolutely that he's always right, smarter than everyone else, and always entitled to the biggest share. This belief made him forever discontent and resentful in life. But he has forgotten now. God bless you Tom.

I've found that Life gives each of us a set of challenges, along with ample opportunities to overcome them, but often it may take more than one lifetime.

My own path has been illogical, improbable, sometimes tragic and very painful, but more often wonderful. I've come to respect it as my own, and I'm grateful for it. I've found that for me, it's best not to insist on a rigid plan. Things work better when I follow where my heart goes, usually off the beaten track, where everybody tells me I shouldn't go. I do it anyway because I've got to care where I go, *me– not them,* though I know they mean well.

I value my practical mind for the useful tool it is, and I

don't leave home without it. But I put my heart out in front of me like a compass, so that even in the times when I can't see beyond my own footsteps, I can still keep going in the direction where it leads me, and it has never led me wrong.

41. We Who Have Come Here

All who come here, go. We all die. That's the price we pay for the ride, but it is an awesome ride.

We are always where we were meant to be, and no part of life is without meaning. In every life, there will be an infinite number of roads and crossroads the soul of us can choose, and though we may wander, lose direction, or experience fears and regrets, we are never really lost, even when we think we are. There is no place we will ever come but home, and after we finally have come home, we will all know this.

And then we will set out again and forget what we knew, so that we can learn again in pure innocence from new adventures and discoveries. Every road is open, and every experience holds a gift, though we may not see it at the time, or recognize its value until we are a good way further down the path.

Small things matter. Everything we do in kindness comes back to us – not like a boomerang but usually in another time and place when we need it most. Sometimes what looks like a tragic loss turns out to be a gift in the long run. Something bad may teach us something good, like compassion. Or loss may show us a simpler beauty we didn't see before.

Miracles are everywhere, just look:

The summer rain blesses everything on which it falls, though it travels through nothing but air, from where and what it was, to become the gift it becomes.

Everything matters. Even if in ways we can't see right now, everything blesses something. All life is born in both pain and joy, and also lives that way.

Every year the summer comes like love, as if it had never come before and never would again. And yet again, it does.

About the Author

Victoria Chames is an artist, poet, and essayist living in Northern California and currently working on the trilogy, *Victory Is My Name, a Memoir*

To contact the author:
moreaboutthis@darkhorsepress.com

Darkhorse Press: Write With Spirit.

We are a Small Press in the time-honored tradition of American authors and self-publishers like Henry David Thoreau, Ralph Waldo Emerson, Walt Whitman, and many others. Small Presses and self-publishing have always been a respected part of the American Literature.